To Tom and ♡

Prov. 3:5,6

BATTLE FOR YANGA

BATTLE FOR YANGA

V. Ben Kendrick

Foreword by Mark Jackson

REGULAR BAPTIST PRESS
1300 North Meacham Road
Schaumburg, Illinois 60173-
4888

Library of Congress Cataloging in Publication Data

Kendrick, V   Ben
    The Battle for Yanga

    I.   Title.
PS3561.E2436B37   811'.54   80-20643
ISBN 0-87227-074-2

BATTLE FOR YANGA
© 1980
Regular Baptist Press
Schaumburg, Illinois
Printed in U.S.A.

2d Printing—1983
3d Printing—1988

It is with great joy that I dedicate this book to my Baptist Mid-Missions' co-workers in the Chad Republic and the Central African Republic who were a constant source of encouragement to me as I witnessed their fruitful lives of faithful service.

I also want to take this opportunity to express my appreciation to Shirley Hull, Sallie McElwain, Beth McGrew and Doug Richardson for their help in preparing this manuscript.

Contents

Foreword

What a thrill to be able to write a brief word for the opening pages of the newest book by V. Ben Kendrick, *The Battle for Yanga*. We have been close friends for thirty-five years, and I rejoice at the blessing of the Lord upon him, his ministry and his writings.

In the 1940s we were classmates at Baptist Bible College (then Baptist Bible Seminary, Johnson City, New York), and he was known affectionately as "Benny" to all of us.

Even in those days, the love of and call to missions were predominant in his life, and those of us around him knew that God would use him mightily on the mission field in years to come.

Appointed in 1949 to French Equatorial Africa by Baptist Mid-Missions, he and his wife, Nina, served faithfully for many years in what is now called the Chad Republic and the Central African Republic until Baptist Mid-Missions recognized his unusual abilities and asked him to serve as deputation coordinator in the United States. Now, as a conference speaker, author and servant to many missionaries, his ministry is expanded manyfold.

You'll enjoy this newest book from Brother Kendrick's life and exciting experiences. It, like his others, throbs with the heartbeat of the mission field. You won't be able to put it down until you finish it!

Baptist Bible College is proud to have such an illustrious missionary, author, speaker and mission administrator as an honored alumnus. Our prayer is that his new book will stir your heart and create an even deeper concern for lost men everywhere.

Mark Jackson, President
Baptist Bible College
Clarks Summit, Pennsylvania

Introduction

Reading, said Bacon, makes a full man. He did not go on to explain what he meant by "full." Probably his thought was that reading—good reading—expands knowledge, keeps one informed and makes life a richer experience.

So it does. And this applies in a special way to Christian literature. Reading the Word is the indispensable practice for believers. In addition, reading Christian biographies, Christian narratives and Christian fiction can have profoundly blessed effects. How many have been saved . . . how many have given their lives to Christ . . . how many have been strengthened . . . how many have been comforted . . . all through Christian literature? The number is surely beyond estimate.

Thus it is a pleasure to see this book come into print. Missions-related writing is plentiful, of course. Yet, some areas of the contemporary missionary enterprise have not been well represented. Even fewer in number are well-developed accounts of our brethren in other lands: their lifestyles, their struggles, their problems and their victories in the Lord. This volume relieves that void.

Dr. Kendrick is a veteran missionary and mission board executive. Beyond this, he is a gifted and prolific writer. His earlier work, *Buried Alive for Christ,* has enjoyed a circulation well above the average. And many have testified that God spoke to them through its pages. We trust *The Battle for Yanga* will be likewise fruitful. Regular Baptist Press is pleased to commend it to God's people everywhere. May reading it make you "full" for the Lord Jesus Christ!

Merle R. Hull, Executive Editor
Regular Baptist Press
Schaumburg, Illinois

1
His
Perfect
Timing

"You'll never preach in this village, white man!" spat out the tall African chief. "My people here in Yanga have their own gods, and we do not want to hear about yours. Leave us alone!"

Paul Davis shivered as the chills raced up his backbone. His knees felt more like rubber than flesh and bones. He looked into the expressionless face of his traveling companion, Pastor Kondo, hoping to get some kind of reaction.

"We'd better do as he says, Mr. Davis. The chief means business. Only bad can come from our staying any longer."

Paul Davis was in his second term of missionary service. He knew the Banda tribesmen well enough to know they meant what they said when they raised their voices as Chief Ngonjo had just done.

"Should I shake his hand, Kondo?" inquired the missionary of his African friend who was already on his way to the pickup.

"No, Mr. Davis. Do not say or do a thing. Just follow me. For some reason, this village is extremely antagonistic to the gospel, and we must approach the people very carefully."

The young missionary followed several yards behind his friend as they made their way to the waiting vehicle. The two rode in silence for several minutes before Pastor Kondo spoke.

"I've never seen any of our chiefs respond as Chief Ngonjo just did. Something is terribly wrong, Mr. Davis. Many of my people know I'm a Christian, and I have spoken with many chiefs before, including Chief Ngonjo, but I've never heard anything like that! He isn't a very pleasant man to begin with, and when he gets angry, I don't know of anyone in our tribe who can be compared with him."

Paul swerved to miss a root sticking up in the road as Kondo continued. "I sure wish I knew a better way to approach the chief."

"I do, too, Kondo. We need to pray for him and his people. God can break down that wall of opposition. We both can testify to that because of what He's done in our lives."

"You're right, Mr. Davis! It makes me shudder when I think how I used to make sacrifices with goats and chickens. The change in my life has been a tremendous one. I can hardly believe I am what I am today."

"That's what God does for us, Kondo. He makes us new creatures in Christ when He saves us. He did it for us, and He can do it for Chief Ngonjo too. If only we could present the gospel to him."

"When we get back to the village, Mr. Davis, I'm going to get the Christians together and pray especially for Chief Ngonjo and the village of Yanga. We have a powerful God, and He works through prayer."

"Yes, He does, Kondo. Well, here we are. Come on down to the house with me. I want to give you your Bible lesson that I corrected this morning."

As they entered the driveway of the mission station, Pastor Kondo was the first to spot the blue pickup truck parked beside the Davis home.

"It looks like you have company, Mr. Davis."

"It sure does, Kondo. It's Dr. Simms. I wonder if anything is wrong."

Becky Davis appeared on the front veranda with Ken and Marge Simms just as Paul and Pastor Kondo pulled up alongside the house.

"Hi, Ken! Hi, Marge! This is a pleasant surprise. It's good to see you. Anything wrong down country?"

"Everything's just fine," answered the missionary doctor as he and Paul shook hands. "We wrote you about a month ago that we were planning to pay you and Becky a visit, but Becky says you never received our letter."

"That's par for the course, Ken," laughed Paul. "I don't even like to think about how much of our mail is not reaching us. I'm sure anything that looks interesting or suspicious is opened by the postal authorities."

"We sent a telegram too," added Marge, "but Becky tells us you didn't receive that either."

"Well, it's good to have you with us," said Paul, placing his hand on Ken's shoulder.

Pastor Kondo, standing nearby waiting for the missionaries to end their greetings, reached out and shook Ken's hand. "My eyes are happy to see you, Dr. Simms. I'm walking now as good as new."

The African Christian showed a long scar on his leg where Ken had operated ten months before to set a compound fracture.

"It looks good, Kondo. You're very fortunate. That was a bad break," responded the doctor.

"Thank the Lord you were here. The Lord timed your coming perfectly," Kondo continued.

Ken smiled at his African friend. "God's timing is always perfect, Kondo."

"Yes, it is," replied the young preacher, slowly nodding his head as though deep in thought. "I'm sure there's more to your visit this time, too, than just spending a few days of rest with your co-workers."

Kondo turned to Paul. "If you'll get that lesson for me, Mr. Davis, I will be on my way home. I'm sure Tessi has my meal waiting for me."

"I'll get it," said Paul, turning to go into the house.

"Oh, by the way, Kondo," said Becky, "before Dr. and Mrs. Simms return down country, we want you and Tessi to come and have a meal with us. Just let me know when it's best for you."

"Thank you, Mrs. Davis. We'll let you know," answered the pleased African.

Paul came out of the house with the lesson in his hand. "Only three more to go, Kondo, and you'll finish the book of Ephesians."

"It's been a great study," smiled Kondo. "I'm glad you brought those lessons with you when you returned from America, Mr. Davis. Well, I'd better be going. I'll see you tomorrow."

Kondo turned to leave, then stopped and turned around to face the missionaries again. "About our conversation on the road, Mr. Davis, I will call the Christians together tonight to pray for Chief Ngonjo and his people. I've got a feeling deep within that we're going to see God work a miracle for us. I really believe it!"

As Pastor Kondo spoke, the missionaries could see the confidence in his face. How it thrilled their hearts to see the faith of African believers.

That evening as the two couples sat around the table, Paul told them of his encounter with Chief Ngonjo.

"Maybe we could drive over and see him tomorrow, Paul," spoke Ken. "I have some medicines with me. You know there are always physical needs among these people, and treating them for their physical needs many times opens the door to deal with their spiritual needs as well."

"You're so right, Ken," answered Paul. "Who knows? Maybe the Lord sent you just to open that village to the gospel. Wouldn't that be wonderful?"

Ken could not help but think of Kondo's comment just a few hours earlier.

2
God's Hand at Work

The next afternoon the two men and their wives drove to Yanga. Upon entering the village, Paul noticed a large crowd gathered around the chief's hut, located in the center of the community.

"Something's wrong," he said, stepping down from the truck. "Someone must be sick."

The two missionary men walked slowly to the edge of the crowd. A sea of angry faces turned to meet them.

"What's wrong?" Paul called out. "I've come back to see Chief Ngonjo. Dr. Simms is here with me to treat any who are sick."

"You lie!" someone shouted from the crowd. "You know our chief is sick, and you've come to make fun of our sorrow. Go back to your village. Leave us alone!"

Some of the men moved toward Paul and Ken, threatening them. The two missionaries stood their ground.

"I wouldn't lie to you people," Paul continued. "I've come to help you. My wife and I have come to your land to live among you—to tell you of God's love for you."

A tall man with a piece of bark cloth wrapped around him limped over to the Americans. "What good is your God's love when our chief is sick? We want him to get better. We don't want to sit here and listen to your words."

"Where is the chief?" asked Paul. "If he is sick, Dr. Simms should see him immediately. I'm sure he can help."

Without questioning Paul's words any further, some of the villagers led the two men into the large hut. Smoke and darkness made it impossible to see anything, and the missionaries found themselves stumbling over people sitting on the floor. A kerosene lantern was lit, revealing the form of a man on a grass mat in the center of the mud-block structure. A few red coals were smoldering beside him, sending smoke upward to cover the already blackened bamboos which supported the grass roof.

"Chief," Paul whispered, "we've come to help you. I brought Dr. Simms with me, and he wants to examine you."

The chief was burning with fever. Every now and then he would cry out. The two men immediately recognized that he was delirious and unaware of their presence.

"I believe it's malaria, Paul," Ken said. "Bring me the ice thermos from the truck. I have something here in my bag that I can give him."

Within minutes Ken had injected the medicine into the chief. Some of the Africans groaned as they saw the needle thrust into their leader's body. A wave of whispering was heard from those who were seated nearby.

Paul returned with the ice cubes, and they were soon wrapped in a cloth and placed on the chief's forehead. Within minutes the sick man began to stir. In a short time he was fully conscious and talking to those around him.

"What are these men doing here?" he asked, lifting his heavy arms to point at Paul and Ken who were kneeling beside him.

"We came to see you, Chief Ngonjo," answered Paul. "It looks like we came just in time. You had a very high temperature."

Paul motioned toward his co-worker. "This is Dr. Simms, Chief. He's the one who's just given you medicine to help you."

"I knew I was sick yesterday when you were here," said the village leader, looking at Paul. "I wanted you to leave so I could make a sacrifice to my gods. I didn't want to make them angrier."

The chief paused to catch his breath. "After you left, I made a sacrifice on that altar there by the door, but my gods either didn't hear me or they didn't want to help. Instead of getting better, I got worse."

He stopped to get his breath. "Even though I chased you and your God away, you came back. Why?"

"Our God sent us back to you, Chief. He knew you needed help. He sent us to help you," Paul answered.

The chief closed his eyes and slowly shook his head back and forth, indicating his amazement at the presence of the two missionaries.

"Chief Ngonjo," Ken said in a soft voice, "I think you should go to the mission station with us. You need more medicine by injection. Since I'm the only one around to give you the injections, I'm asking you to go back with us. In another hour you should be well enough to travel that far."

"If your God tells you that, I'll go back with you. Your God makes you and your medicine powerful. My gods have failed me."

Again the men could hear the people in the hut whisper to each other, surprised at their leader's words. There was no doubt among them that their chief was fighting a real battle in his heart. His disappointment in his gods clearly showed in his actions as well as his words.

Outside, Becky and Marge were busy making a comfortable bed in the back of the truck for their very special patient. Ken asked several of the men to carry their leader to the truck. The missionary doctor then climbed into the back of the vehicle so he would be close to his precious cargo.

The trip to the station was uneventful. Within a half hour they were turning down the driveway and heading toward the recently completed building used for sick people who required treatment for a period of time. The three-room apartment was like a palace compared to any of the African homes. The attractive rooms with their whitewashed walls and ceiling impressed the chief.

"This is a nice house, Mr. Davis," the village leader said as he was helped into the building. "You are kind to me."

"Please believe me, Chief, when I tell you that it is a joy to do this for you. You see, our God loves you, and we want you to know and love Him as we do."

The sick African seemed to close his ears to the missionary's words. Paul and Ken sensed the battle going on within the African's heart, but already they could see a change in his attitude.

"I know it's still early, Chief," said Ken, "but you need your rest, so I'm putting you to bed. I'm going to stay in the next room tonight, so don't worry about a thing. If you need me, I'm here to help."

Chief Ngonjo tried to force a smile. "I can't understand you people. You are so good to me when I haven't done anything good for you. In fact, if I could have killed Mr. Davis yesterday, I would have done so."

Paul, standing silently by, looked a bit surprised. A chill ran up his spine. He hadn't known he had been in such great danger. Now he realized why Pastor Kondo had told him to leave without shaking hands or saying another word.

"Thank You, Lord, for Pastor Kondo and his love for us," he whispered. "Thank You for sparing my life yesterday."

"Well, Chief Ngonjo," said Paul, shaking the sick man's hand, "you need to rest, so I'll say good night. I'll see you in the morning."

"Good night, Mr. Davis. Thank you for coming back today."

The African's words struck a chord in Paul's heart, sending mixed feelings racing through his mind. As he left the building, his eyes became moist as he thought of Chief Ngonjo and his need for Christ. At the same time, he could not help but rejoice that God had placed the chief within their reach so they might minister to him.

"Father," Paul prayed as he walked up the path to the small mission house, "I believe we see Your hand at work. Thank You for bringing Chief Ngonjo to us. Somehow, Lord, help us to get the gospel message across to him. Bless Ken tonight as he stays with him. Give him the opportunity to witness, Father. May Chief Ngonjo be saved. Dear Father, please open the village of Yanga to the gospel."

Over in the nearby workmen's village, unknown to the missionaries, Pastor Kondo's house was packed with village Christians. "Father," prayed Kondo, "we have gathered tonight to pray for Chief Ngonjo. He is such a hardhearted man and has so many followers in his village. I am sure, Lord, that if he'd come to know You, his influence would be used by You to bring many of his tribesmen to Christ. Dear Father, spare Chief Ngonjo's life and save him. We're asking You to work a miracle and open the village of Yanga to the gospel."

As Pastor Kondo said amen, all the believers joined their voices with his. There was no doubt in their hearts that God was going to answer their prayers. Little did they realize, however, how sorely their faith would be tried before morning.

3
A
New
Name

Paul Davis had just gone to sleep when a spear came crashing through the window screen, striking the concrete block wall opposite the bed and clanking to the floor. A bloodcurdling yell made the half-dazed missionary sit straight up in bed.

"What was that?" Becky screamed, slipping out of bed and pulling on her robe.

"Get down on the floor and don't move!" shouted Paul as he ran to the window to close the board shutters.

In the moonlight he saw a group of men standing in the front yard. He was careful not to shine his flashlight in any of their faces, thinking it might disturb them even more.

"Who is it? What do you want?" called Paul, trying to get a glimpse of their faces.

"It's me, Kota. Ngonjo's brother. I've come to get him and take him home."

"You can't do that, Kota," reasoned the missionary from the window. "He's being treated by Dr. Simms."

"You're lying, white man. You can't fool us. You've brought him here to make him even sicker and possibly even kill him."

Paul recognized the spokesman as the man from Yanga with a limp who had been dressed in bark cloth.

"You're mistaken, my friend. Your brother is over in that house with Dr. Simms." Paul pointed the beam of light toward the newly constructed building.

Marge Simms had been awakened by the commotion and had hurried to the Davis's bedroom door. Becky, hearing her knock, quickly opened the door and pulled Marge to the floor beside her.

"It's Chief Ngonjo's brother, Marge," whispered Becky. "He thinks we have harmed his brother and has come to get him."

The three missionaries were startled but relieved to hear a familiar voice call out from the darkness across the mission station. "Stop right where you are. Put down those weapons."

"It's Pastor Kondo!" whispered Paul.

"Mr. Davis! Are you all right?"

"We're OK, Kondo. The spear just made a hole in the screen. It didn't hurt us."

Pastor Kondo appeared in the beam of the flashlight, followed by about twenty men.

"Why, you're the one who came with the white man two days ago," Kota called. "Why take his side? You're one of us."

"These are my friends. They are here to help all of us. We're here to protect them and their property."

Before another word was spoken, the cry of "fire" was heard from the mission village where Paul's workmen lived. One of Kota's men had slipped over to the village and had set fire to three of the believers' houses. The flames quickly soared into the dark sky as the dry grass roofs ignited like torches. Kondo turned toward the village with a surprised look on his face.

"All right, you traitor," called Kota, "let's see you defend your missionaries while your houses burn."

Two of the men rushed at Kondo with their knives raised high, only to be stopped in their tracks by a booming voice.

"What is going on here, Kota?"

Chief Ngonjo stepped from the front door of the small house and started across the yard. Dr. Simms was close behind.

"We've come to save you from these people, Ngonjo," answered Kota.

"You've come to save who from these people? What do you think they're doing to me, anyway? I am here because I want to be here!"

The chief turned toward the nearly destroyed houses. "Who started those fires? Did my men do that, Kota?"

The chief's brother then told how they thought the missionaries meant to do harm to their leader. He related how they made plans back in their village to come at night, burn the workmen's village, destroy the mission property and even harm the missionaries.

The chief listened quietly until Kota finished speaking. In great distress, he hung his head for a moment, then looked up.

"Mr. Davis, I'm sorry for this outrage tonight. Pastor Kondo, I know your people suffered great losses. I promise that those houses will be rebuilt by my people. We'll bring the grass and bamboo. We'll also replace anything else destroyed by the fire. When we sell our cotton crop in a few days, we'll have sufficient money to rebuild and replace everything. I promise."

As everyone stood speechless, the village leader turned to his brother.

"Kota, I am ordering you and these men to go with Pastor Kondo right now and clean up the debris from the fires. When you are finished, return to Yanga. I'll send you further orders tomorrow."

Not yet finished speaking, Chief Ngonjo turned to Kondo. "These men are yours to do with as you please. Keep them until you are satisfied that your village is as clean as it can be. You will also have charge of them when they rebuild your houses."

Without another word, the men set off in the direction of the workmen's village. Everything had happened so quickly that the missionaries were dazed. The two couples spoke briefly in the front yard while the chief waited nearby. Ken excused himself, realizing he still had a very sick patient. He and the chief returned to the small house. Paul, Becky and Marge were so wide awake that they sat and talked until almost daybreak.

The early morning sun cast a sliver of light on Ken's face. He opened his eyes and looked around. Quickly he remembered where he was and the fearful events of the past night. His attention shifted to his patient in the next room as he listened to the systematic rhythm of the snoring made by the chief. He slowly got out of bed and quietly walked to the doorway.

"Wake up, Chief," Ken called softly.

The African continued to snore.

"It's time to get up, Chief. Are you ready for breakfast?"

"Breakfast!" Chief Ngonjo sat up and swung his legs over the side of the bed.

"Hey! Take it easy," cautioned Ken. "Remember, you're a sick man."

"I feel like a new man, doctor," answered the African with a grin. "Your God knows all about me. He made me well."

"He made your body well, Chief," continued the doctor, "but He hasn't made your heart well yet."

"He will," said the chief, not realizing what Ken meant. "He knows all about me. Listen, doctor, while I tell you what He has done for me."

Ken sat down beside the chief and listened intently to what his friend had to say.

"First of all," he said, holding up one finger, "He sent you to visit Mr. Davis. Second, He knew I was sick and was beyond the help of my gods. Third, He put it in your hearts to come to my village even though I told Mr. Davis to stay away from us. Fourth, He used you to make me well. And fifth," he continued, pointing to his thumb for the number five, "He told you to bring me here so you could help me. Doctor, your God is wise and powerful. You missionaries must really be afraid of Him to obey Him the way you do."

"Oh, no, Chief," answered Ken with his broad smile. "It's not that we're afraid of Him. You see, Chief, we love Him. We love Him with all our hearts. He gave us eternal life and has forgiven our sins."

"He's done what?" asked the chief with a questioning look.

"He gave me eternal life. I'm going to live forever, Chief. Let me tell you about Him while the coffee water is heating."

The missionary doctor began by telling how man sinned, thus separating himself from God. He told how the Father, in His great love, sent His Son, Jesus, to die for the sins of the world. He then explained the necessity of accepting Christ as Savior. As he neared the end of the story of the cross, the excited chief interrupted him.

"You mean that's what Mr. Davis has been trying to tell us? Is that the reason for his coming to my village and accepting my insults without getting angry with me? Do you mean to say that he's returned good for evil just because he wanted to tell me about Jesus? Is that why he left his country and came this long way to live among us?"

"That's right, Chief Ngonjo. That's why he and Mrs. Davis left their home to come and live among you and your people."

The chief looked overwhelmed at what he had heard. "Doctor, I want to accept Jesus as you told me in your story, just like you men have done. I want Him to live in my heart. I do not want to serve my gods any longer."

The burdened chief laid his head on his knees. "Help me, doctor. Help me know this Jesus."

The two men bowed their heads as the African confessed his sins and asked Christ to save him. When he finished praying, he reached out and shook Ken's hand.

"My heart thanks you, doctor. Now I want you to give me a new name."

"A new what?" Ken asked, looking at the chief with a puzzled face.

"A new name, doctor," answered the smiling African. "You see, the name 'Ngonjo' means anger and hatred. I do not want that name anymore. What should I be called?"

"Well," said the missionary, looking into the face of the new-born Christian, "why don't you take the name of Paul? Chief Paul. That's a good name."

"But that's what you call Mr. Davis!" spoke the African.

"Yes, that's his name, but I'm sure he won't mind. Take the name of Paul and, as we have our coffee, I'll read you a story about Paul from God's Word, the Bible. He also received the name of Paul after he accepted Jesus as His Savior."

The door opened and Paul Davis entered the room. "Good morning, Ken. Good morning, Chief Ngonjo. How are you feeling this morning?"

"I am not Ngonjo anymore," laughed the African. "I'm Chief Paul. God gave me a new name. He did it through the doctor."

"I don't understand," Paul Davis said with a confused look.

Ken stood up, laughing. "The chief has accepted Jesus as his Savior and he asked me to give him a new name. He said the old name meant—"

"It meant anger and hatred," interrupted Paul. "He sure fit his name too," he added, jokingly.

"Those are true words, Mr. Davis. You are fortunate you're saying it now. I don't know what I would have done with you in the village if you had said it then." ·

"Thank the Lord, Chief Paul. That name sure sounds a lot better."

"The doctor told me that another man who accepted Jesus as his Savior also received the name of Paul. He is going to read me the story from God's Word, the Bible, while we drink our coffee."

Chief Paul looked up at Paul and smiled.

"Sit down, Mr. Davis. There's an extra cup here, and besides, you do want to hear why you got your name, don't you?"

The three men looked at each other and laughed. Truly this was a time for rejoicing. Chief Paul's village would soon be a main preaching center for the gospel.

4

The
Grim
Reminder

The next several days saw some wonderful things happen. Chief Paul responded to Dr. Simms' treatment and was able to return to his village to supervise the sale of his people's cotton crop. He insisted that the two missionary couples return with him.

"This is the best cotton crop we have had in many years," said the chief to his missionary friends as they stood together under a shade tree.

"How much cotton do you think is in these baskets, Chief?" Ken asked, pointing to the rows of cotton-filled baskets running the length of the village.

"Well, their average weight is 150 pounds, so we must have about nine tons of cotton this year."

"That's wonderful, Chief," responded Ken, gazing at the rows of baskets.

"You don't know it," said the chief with a grin, "but my people who have already been paid for their cotton have contributed to the rebuilding of those three houses in the workmen's village." Chief Paul then motioned for them to follow him. "Come with me. I want to show you something."

The missionaries were led to a little, hastily built shelter where a pail was sitting in the middle of a small table.

"That's our collection for the construction as well as for the replacement of the contents of the houses of the three families."

As Chief Paul spoke, a man walked up to the table and dropped several paper bills into the nearly full pail.

"What if you get too much, Chief?" asked Becky, smiling.

"Well, in that case, Mrs. Davis, we've decided to buy Pastor

Kondo a new bicycle. He hasn't said anything to you, I'm sure, but his bicycle is very old and doesn't have much more use in it."

Paul stood shaking his head. "This is unbelievable. It hardly seems possible that less than a week ago I stood here with my life threatened. Now here I am by the invitation of the same man who wanted to kill me!"

"God did it, Mr. Davis," Chief Paul replied. "My heart is happy. I do not hate anymore."

"It's a miracle, Chief Paul," said Marge.

"Yes, it's a miracle. But oh, how I want that same miracle to happen to my brother, Kota."

The chief stopped talking because of the choked-up feeling in his throat.

"We know how you feel, Chief," said Paul, "and we'll pray for Kota. God can save him too."

"Ngonjo, uh—uh—Paul!" called Kota, coming into the back of the village from a small path leading out of the cotton gardens. "We probably have twenty more baskets left and that's all for this year's crop."

"That's good, Kota," answered his brother. "Come here and count this money. It looks like we'll be able to get that bicycle for Kondo after all."

"Ngonjo, uh—uh—Paul, I mean, what's wrong with you? Why, I can't believe you're the same man. You would never have done anything like this before you—you went to that mission station."

"You're right, Kota. If Jesus were not my Savior, I would still be the same old hateful, bitter Ngonjo. God has changed me, Kota. I feel like new."

Kota continued to speak to his brother as he counted the money. "But what about us? How's your change going to affect us? You aren't like the rest of us anymore."

"Some of you will soon be changed like me," the chief said with confidence. "The powerful God can save you, too, Kota, but I hope you won't have to get sick for Him to do it."

Paul looked up to see four men carrying a large basket of cotton into the village from the garden patch. "There's another one, Chief Paul. Your people seem happy about this good crop of cotton."

"There's already enough here to buy all that is needed, including the bicycle," said Kota, pointing to the stacks of bills on the ground.

"Good," responded his brother. "That means we can build a meeting place with what is left over."

"What did I hear you say?" exclaimed Kota, somewhat startled.

"A meeting place, Kota. A place where the missionaries or Kondo can come and teach us from God's Book."

"Now I know your head is turned," answered the surprised Kota. "Something terrible has happened to you. A meeting place!" he grunted as he turned away.

The missionaries looked at each other in surprise. None of them had said anything to the chief about a meeting place. "Surely," thought Paul, "the Spirit of God is preparing this man and his village for a great work."

The length of his shadow before him caused Paul Davis to look at his watch. "Say, we must be going if we're going to get home in time for me to clean that carburetor on the light plant!"

The missionaries shook hands with Chief Paul, Kota and several other villagers standing nearby. Ken checked with the chief to make sure he understood when to take the pills he had been given. As they drove out of Yanga, the two couples talked of the week of miracles they had just experienced.

"God has surely answered prayers this week," said Paul, pulling down the sun visor to shield his eyes from the western sun.

"Yes, He has," responded Becky. "Chief Paul's conversion has changed the whole picture."

At the mission station they received another surprise. A crew of men from Yanga had already begun the reconstruction of the destroyed houses. Pastor Kondo, under orders from Chief Paul, was directing the work detail. While Becky and Marge prepared the evening meal, Ken and Paul strolled over to the village to watch the men work.

"It looks good, men," called Paul as he and Ken walked into the village.

"Thank you, sir," one of the men responded.

"All right, men," called Kondo. "It's time to eat."

The hungry crew formed a circle on the ground as a bowl of water was passed around for them to wash their hands. Pastor Kondo then asked the men to bow their heads as he prayed. Even then the wise pastor used the opportunity to let the men know they were sinners, and that God loved them and sent His Son to die for them. Several repeated the amen after Kondo. The women then brought the bowls of cooked rice and chicken. One by one the men broke off a handful of rice and dipped it into the chicken gravy. The loud smacking of lips told everyone within hearing distance that the food was good.

Paul and Ken turned quietly to return to the house.

"Mister! Can I speak with you?"

They were surprised to see one of the men from Yanga stand up and walk over to them.

"He's probably not feeling well," whispered Paul, "and wants some medicine from you."

"What can we do for you?" Paul asked the khaki-clad young man.

"I know this sounds strange, but I talked with our chief before you took him home today. He told me about my sinful heart and how Jesus can make it clean. He has happiness and peace in his heart now, and, mister, I too want that kind of heart."

Paul spoke quietly to the African, explaining the plan of salvation.

"And that's all there is to it, Kolo. Jesus died for you and will give you eternal life if you will accept Him."

Within minutes, right there on the path, Kolo prayed, confessing his sins and asking Christ to become his Savior. Paul was so thrilled about the young man's conversion that he asked Kolo to come to the house so Becky and Marge could hear the good news from the new believer's own lips.

As the two couples sat at the dinner table that evening, they were still bubbling over the conversion of Kolo.

"And to think," said Ken, "that this is a direct result of Chief Paul's witness. Another miracle of the Lord."

Later that night, as Paul opened the board shutters in the bedroom, he noticed the spear hole in the screen. He turned to look in the corner of the room. There, standing forgotten by all, was the seven-foot spear, a grim reminder of what could have happened had God not intervened.

5

'O Death,
Where
Is Thy
Sting?'

Marge Simms dabbed at her eyes with the small white handkerchief she clutched in her right hand. "We really don't want to go
back home, Becky. These past two weeks have been two of the
most wonderful weeks Ken and I have experienced here in Africa."

She looked out over the large crowd of Africans who had
gathered on the front yard of the Davis home. "Look over there,
Becky. Just look at Chief Paul. What a great, wonderful change has
taken place in that man's life."

Becky Davis smiled as she glanced in the direction of the new
Christian. He was the center of attention as he recounted what
took place the night that some of his men came to "rescue" him
from the missionaries. Paul and Ken stood laughing as the old chief
acted out the scene.

"I thought I was dreaming when I heard Kota's voice. How I
ever got to the door without Dr. Simms seeing me, I'll never know.
Once I saw what was going on here in this yard, I knew it wasn't a
dream. Dr. Simms awoke just then and told me to stay in the house,
but it was too late. I was on my way. I knew I had to stop my men
from hurting anyone or destroying the mission station. When Dr.
Simms caught up with me and took me by the arm, I told him I
would just have to drag him with me!"

A roar of laughter went up from the crowd.

"Well, when I saw Kolo and Bimba raise their knives, I knew I'd
better act quickly. It was then that I yelled as loudly as I could."

"You not only stopped them, Chief Paul," called someone

from the crowd, "but you woke up everyone in the two nearby villages too!"

Another burst of laughter went up from the happy gathering.

"Well, good-bye, Chief," Ken said, shaking his hand. "I can't begin to tell you how much this visit has meant to me. You've been a great blessing to my heart."

"Good-bye, Dr. Simms," responded the tall leader. He then took Ken's head gently in his two hands and blew softly into each of the doctor's ears. The Africans stood in silence as they watched the chief's farewell to his American friend.

"Such affection is shown only among the closest of family members in the Banda tribe," Becky whispered to Marge Simms.

Paul Davis then asked Pastor Kondo to pray for their departing friends. Once again the faithful young pastor used the opportunity to present the gospel. Then the blue pickup headed slowly down the mission station driveway and onto the main road. The chief wiped his eyes and looked at Paul.

"I'm going to miss him, Mr. Davis. Not everyone would do for me what he did. I'll never forget how he stayed right with me from the moment we left my house until the next morning. He shows God's love in his actions."

"Yes, he does, Chief Paul. God has given him a heart filled with love and compassion."

"I want you to know, Mr. Davis, that it was that love and compassion for me that finally caused me to listen to what you missionaries were saying."

"By the way, Chief, where's Kota?"

Paul's question caused a look of disappointment to appear on the African's face.

"Kota went hunting today. He says a stray buffalo has been getting into his garden, so he went out to try to kill it."

"Aren't they dangerous, Chief? I hear that buffaloes kill people around here every year."

"They're dangerous, all right, Mr. Davis. Last year two of my men were gored to death just outside the village."

Changing the subject as he gazed at the shadows made from the afternoon sun, the chief continued: "I think it's time for me to get back to the village. I was going to visit some of the families in the workmen's village, but something tells me I should return to Yanga." A puzzled look was on the leader's face.

Paul expertly guided his truck with its load of Africans along the narrow road. Two miles from Yanga, the chief spotted a runner coming toward them.

"It's Ouia. He's one of the men who went with Kota today. I know he has bad news."

The missionary brought his truck to a stop as Ouia ran to the open cab window. Rivulets of perspiration coursed down his body, saturating his khaki shorts.

"What's wrong, Ouia?" asked Chief Paul, showing concern in the tone of his voice. "Has something happened at Yanga?"

"It's Kota, Chief. A buffalo gored him and he's badly hurt."

"Get in quickly, Ouia," called the missionary. "We must hurry."

The pickup practically flew over the dirt road, leaving a long cloud of dust behind. In a short time the truck pulled into the village of Yanga.

"We may be too late," the chief called as he stepped to the ground. "I hear the death wail coming from that house."

The tall respected leader ran to a nearby hut which was surrounded by people. He entered quickly and immediately spotted his brother lying on the grass mat in the center of the building. He raised his hand and the wailing inside the hut immediately ceased. He then knelt beside Kota who was lying still, his eyes closed. Blood stains were visible on the clay floor, the mat and Kota's clothing. Chief Paul bent low over his brother, looking into his face.

"Kota, can you hear me?" he asked.

The injured African slowly opened his bloodshot eyes and tried to move his lips, but no sound came. The chief then noticed a deep gash in Kota's neck.

"He can't speak," he whispered to Paul, who was standing nearby, "but I believe he can hear me."

Again he spoke to his brother. "Kota, if you hear me, close your eyes."

Slowly the African's eyes closed, then reopened.

Paul tried to determine the extent of Kota's injuries. He couldn't believe the severe damage done to the man by the angered buffalo. Kota's left leg had a compound fracture right below the knee. The wound in his neck was deep and affected not only Kota's voice, but also his breathing. The injury that caused him the most concern, however, was the huge opening in Kota's abdomen which exposed his intestines. Paul had heard of cases where the intestines were pushed back into the body after a battle with a buffalo. There was no doubt in his mind that this was what had happened to Kota.

"Kota," Chief Paul continued, "I'm going to talk to you about something very important. I want you to listen carefully to every word. If you understand what I just said, close your eyes."

Again the dying African slowly closed and opened his eyes.

"I believe God gave you this opportunity to hear about and accept Jesus, Kota. You know how I've told you that He loves you and died to pay the penalty for your sins. Kota," pleaded the chief, "please ask Jesus to become your Savior. Ask Him to forgive you of your sins and trust Him now. If you will do that, Kota, close your eyes so I can know."

Chief Paul sighed with relief as his brother slowly closed his eyes. They remained closed for about a minute and then opened. Kota tried to smile, but only a slight trace of it could be seen on his face.

"Is Jesus in your heart, Kota? Do you belong to Him?"

The chief clasped Kota's hand as his eyes slowly closed again. He tried to open them again, but they only opened part way and then closed. Kota was Home with the Lord.

All was quiet within the hut. No one moved or spoke. Finally, Chief Paul stood to his feet.

"My brother is with Jesus. You have all witnessed his physical death, but the most important thing is that you also have witnessed his birth into God's family. I don't want any wailing. My heart is sad, but the sadness is overshadowed by happiness. I will see Kota again someday in God's house."

Preparations for the funeral were made quickly. Chief Paul asked Pastor Kondo to direct the service at nine o'clock the next morning. Paul Davis returned home as soon as possible to break the news of Kota's acceptance of Christ and his death.

The following morning the entire population of the workmen's village was in Yanga. Most walked a good share of the night to get there. Hundreds came from other nearby villages.

The grave was dug at one end of the village under a flamboyant tree. Kota's body was enclosed in a white wooden box. It was wide enough for the shoulders at one end and narrow at the other end for the feet. The grave was just big enough for the box to stand on end in a tilted position, according to the tribal burial custom.

Kondo opened the service with the singing of two hymns. He

then asked his missionary friend, Paul Davis, to tell of Kota's conversion. The Scriptures were then opened and the pastor spoke about the resurrection from 1 Corinthians 15.

" 'O death,' " Pastor Kondo called out, " 'where is thy sting? O grave, where is thy victory?' " A smile appeared on his face as he concluded, " 'Thanks be to God, which giveth us the victory through our Lord Jesus Christ.' "

At the close of the message, Pastor Kondo gave an invitation, asking the unsaved to accept Christ. As he prayed, thirty-seven people stepped out of the crowd and came forward to be saved. Chief Paul could hardly believe his eyes when Kondo finished praying.

The tall leader stepped forward and raised his hand. "Let's sing one more song. Pastor Kondo, lead us in that song about the names being called in God's house."

Kondo smiled as he raised his arms to lead the group. Tears came to Becky's eyes as she listened to the blend of voices.

> When the trumpet of the Lord shall sound
>   and time shall be no more,
> And the morning breaks eternal, bright and fair—
> When the saved of earth shall gather
>   over on the other shore,
> And the roll is called up yonder—I'll be there!
>
> When the roll is called up yonder,
> When the roll is called up yonder,
> When the roll is called up yonder—
> When the roll is called up yonder I'll be there!

The people then returned to the center of the village where the Christians dealt with those who made decisions.

"Today has been a good day for Yanga, Mr. Davis," Chief Paul said, shaking the missionary's hand. "I know God has many more wonderful things ahead for us. The past two weeks have been hard, but I'm thankful for them." The chief hesitated and then continued. "I really mean it, Mr. Davis, when I say I'm glad for all that has happened at Yanga."

Paul reached out and took his wife's hand. "Thank the Lord that He has allowed us to be a part of it all too."

6
A
Preacher
in the
Family

The morning sun peeking over the distant horizon sent a narrow beam of light across the darkened hut. Tene looked up from his grass mat and watched the tiny particles of dust floating along the illuminated path, beginning with the small hole in the grass room and ending at the base of the far wall.

"Time to get up," the young African whispered to himself. His conversation with Chief Paul the night before was fresh in his mind, and he was anxious to pursue the subject. Tene quickly dressed and made his way to a nearby stream where he took his morning bath. As he splashed the cold water over himself, he thought of the recent happenings in the village of Yanga and the unbelievable changes in the lives of many of the villagers, including his own. He recalled the night that he, along with a number of other men led by Kota, made an attack on the Davis house at the mission station. A chill ran through Tene's body as he thought of his part in it. How thankful he was that his spear had passed over the missionaries as they were in bed and hit the far wall of the bedroom.

"Thank You, Father," he breathed, "for causing that spear to miss them."

Tene had accepted Christ at Kota's funeral a few weeks later. After the service he told Paul Davis that he was the one who had thrown the spear through the bedroom window. He recalled how the missionary reached out and put his arm around him.

"Don't feel bad about it," Paul had said. "You were doing what you thought you had to do to rescue your chief. And besides," he had continued, "the thing that really counts is that you are now my brother in Christ."

Tene made his way back to his hut and then started to make breakfast for himself. He crushed some dried coffee beans and put them into a pot of water which was boiling over a small fire in his front yard. Reaching up to the low grass roof, he pulled loose two dried ears of corn which he shoved into the coals of the hot fire. He was just about to go back into his hut when he heard Chief Paul's voice.

"Good morning, Tene. How are you today?"

"I'm fine, Chief," responded the thin African lad.

"Do you mind if I sit down with you?" asked the village leader as he reached out to shake Tene's hand.

"Do sit down, Chief. If you have not eaten yet, why not eat with me?"

"I will if I'm not making you short on food." The chief knew that many of the single young men of the village ate very sparingly since they did not have wives to make gardens and cook their food for them.

Tene hurried into the hut to get the two cans of sardines he had saved for such a special guest. He quickly washed and dried two aluminum plates which he had tucked away in a suitcase hanging from one of the bamboo supports holding up the grass roof—the best place to put it so the termites couldn't get it. In a few minutes he joined the chief outside the hut.

"Like I told you last night, Chief," spoke Tene, sitting down on a small hand-carved stool, "I have had several years of training in our district school. I can read and write. I would like to go to Bible school."

"You say you have spoken with Mr. Davis about this?" questioned the village leader.

"Yes, I have. Two weeks after I was saved I asked him if I could become a pastor like Pastor Kondo."

"If that is what God wants you to be, Tene, then you have my support as chief of this village." Chief Paul smiled at the excited young man and continued. "You will be the first one from our village to train for God's work. I'm sure the Christians here at Yanga will give money to help you. They will be proud to have one of their own men in Bible school."

Tene was so overwhelmed he could hardly eat his corn and sardines. "Just think," he said to himself, "I am going to Bible school! I will be able to be a pastor right here among my own people!"

Chief Paul seemed to sense the young man's thoughts and reached over and placed his hand on Tene's shoulder. "I believe God has a great work for you, Tene. Your father and mother would be proud of you if they were living today. In fact, the day before they died in the grass fire, they spoke of how they wanted you to grow up and be a help to your own people." The chief hesitated a moment. "Since they were not Christians, I know they never thought of you as being a preacher."

Tene's eyes filled with tears as he listened to his chief. His thoughts raced back to that terrible day in his life.

"I am adopting you, Tene, as my own son." Chief Paul's words came as a shock to the young man. Tene could hold back the tears no longer. He bowed his head and cried quietly. Chief Paul's strong arm tightened about his shoulders.

"Thank you, Chief Paul. Thank you very much," Tene finally said. "I will try to be a good son for you."

Paul and Becky Davis stopped in Yanga that afternoon as they were returning from a two-day trip among the villages. As they stepped from the truck, Tene appeared in front of them.

"Hello, Mr. Davis. Hello, Mrs. Davis. My eyes are happy to see you again."

"Hello, Tene," answered Paul, shaking the young man's hand. "It's good to see you again too."

"Hello, Mr. Davis," called Chief Paul, coming around the corner of his hut. "You must have heard the good news."

"No, I haven't, Chief. What good news are you talking about?"

Tene turned to the chief. "I have not said anything to them about it, Papa. I wanted you to tell them."

"Papa?" said the missionary with a questioning look on his face. "Did I hear correctly, Chief?"

"Your ears have heard right, Mr. Davis. I am making a legal request with the government to adopt Tene. According to our tribal laws, he is already my son."

"That's wonderful!" exclaimed Becky, clapping her hands with excitement. "I can hardly believe all that's happened here in Yanga since you were saved, Chief."

"But there is something else we want to tell you," said Chief Paul, a smile spreading across his scarred face.

"I don't know if I can take any more, Chief," Paul replied.

"You know that Tene has been talking about Bible school," Chief Paul began. "Now we want to tell you that he is ready to leave for school. Will you talk with the director of the school? Tene wants to become a pastor here among his own people."

Praise the Lord!" shouted Paul as he vigorously shook Tene's hand. The excitement that followed brought the villagers running to see what had happened.

The missionary turned to the village chief. "You see, Chief Paul, all things do work together for good. You were ill, but through it you came to know Jesus. Your men burned three homes in the workmen's village, but while they were rebuilding the houses, Kolo and a number of others accepted Jesus. Kota was saved before he died, and even his death was used by God to bring over thirty of your people to accept Jesus."

Paul Davis then faced Tene. "And here is one of those who accepted Christ that day beside your brother's grave. Only the Lord knew that the same young man who threw the spear through our window that night would stand one day before the people of Yanga, declaring himself as a candidate for Bible school."

Paul stepped toward the chief and shook his hand. "You've not only gained a son today, Chief, but you have also invited a preacher into your family."

Chief Paul's face shone with happiness as he stood with his arm around his adopted son.

7

The Underground Safe

Pastor Kondo looked across the yard at his new bicycle leaning against a mango tree. The shiny red paint seemed to be even brighter than the day before. The African pastor walked over to the bicycle and gently ran his hand over the chrome handlebars.

"Thank You, Father, for giving me this bicycle. Thank You for putting the need for it in Chief Paul's heart."

As he stood alongside his valuable possession, Kondo became lost in his thoughts. He thought of the many things that had happened the past two months. It seemed like only yesterday— even though two weeks had gone by—since Paul Davis had shared the good news with him that Chief Paul had adopted Tene and that the young man felt the call of God to go to Bible school.

"Father," prayed the African pastor in a whisper, "thank You for saving Tene and for putting it in his heart to go to Bible school."

"Pastor! Are you going to the farewell service?"

Kondo looked up to see one of the older men of the workmen's village walking toward him.

"Yes, I'm going, Douyou. I've been lost in thought about all that has happened around here lately." Kondo threw his leg over the bicycle. "It will take me awhile to get there, so I'd better be going. Thank you, Douyou, for waking me up."

"Well, I can understand, Pastor, why you do get lost in your thoughts. A lot has happened around here. I have known Chief Ngonjo, uh—uh—Paul, for many years, and the miracle in his life alone is enough for anyone to think about many, many times."

The African pastor reached out to shake the old man's hand. "I'll see you later, Douyou. This is going to be an important farewell service—the village of Yanga sending its first man to Bible school!"

The road to Yanga was difficult in many places because of the deep sand. Normally Kondo would have traveled with Paul and Becky Davis, but the missionary couple had to go to a village beyond Yanga the day before and were planning to stop on their way home.

Kondo had just started moving on his bike again, after carrying it through some sand, when he heard a rustle in the leaves nearby. He swerved, but it was too late. A long, black, spitting cobra darted out from the brush and went headlong into the front spokes of the bicycle.

"Help!" Kondo called as he went sprawling headfirst over the handlebars onto the dusty road. The snake twisted and turned among the spokes, trying to free itself. Kondo got up and ran a short distance to get out of the range of the spitting cobra's venom. In a minute the serpent freed itself and disappeared into the bush. The pastor stood still for a moment and listened to the rustling leaves as the creature entered the forest. He then bowed his head.

"Dear Lord, thank You for sparing my life. Thank You for watching over me."

Thirty minutes later, Kondo rode into the village of Yanga. As he told what had happened to him, the entire village broke into laughter.

"That's the first time I've heard of a snake colliding with a bicycle," Chief Paul laughed.

"Weren't you scared?" asked Becky, trying to hide the grin on her face.

The laughter soon subsided as the seriousness of the occasion took over. The little chapel was packed with people sitting in the aisles as well as lining the outside walls of the building. Chief Paul had worked out the program with Pastor Kondo and Paul Davis. The blend of voices could be heard for a considerable distance as the congregation, led by Kondo, started to sing:

> What can wash away my sin?
> Nothing but the blood of Jesus;
> What can make me whole again?
> Nothing but the blood of Jesus.

"It's time for testimonies, friends," called Chief Paul, directing his part of the program. "I am sure everyone who is saved has some word of praise to our God."

40

One person after another stood up, testifying to what Christ meant to him. An hour later, as Chief Paul was about to close his part of the service, an old woman rose to her feet. As she began to speak, every eye was upon her.

"I don't need to tell you my name. You all know me. I watched many of you grow up from your baby days."

Paul noticed a fearful look in Chief Paul's eyes as he stood listening. He didn't know the old woman was the chief's mother who lived by herself in a hut far off in the forest. Many people said she was possessed with evil spirits, and they were afraid to go anywhere near her hut. As for the chief, he was a regular visitor to see his mother until the day he told her he had burned his gods and had accepted Jesus as his Savior.

"You burned the gods of your fathers for the white man's God!" she had screamed. "You are no longer my son. I do not want you to enter my house again!"

Chief Paul had tried to witness to his mother many times after that, but he was driven away by an avalanche of terrible names. The village leader had been disowned by his own mother.

After pausing to catch her breath, the old woman continued: "I went into the forest and saw Kota's blood on the ground. Then I heard from Ngonjo, or Paul as you call him, how Kota asked Jesus to come into his heart right before he died. I have seen the change in Ngonjo, and I know he is a different man."

As the old woman spoke, no one stirred. It was the first time in years that many of the villagers had heard her speak. Chief Paul, not knowing what to do, decided to let his mother continue.

"Now, my people," she said, placing one hand on her hip and shaking the other hand to emphasize what she was saying, "the God that Ngonjo and Kota accepted must be a powerful God. I was filled with anger and hatred when those boys were born. That is why I named them 'Big-Hatred.' I have been hating most everyone for years—until now. These words which I have heard from my own people this past hour tell me something. What they have in their hearts is real and true."

The crowd buzzed with excitement. The old woman waited for them to quiet down. She turned to look at Tene, who was seated in front between Kondo and Paul Davis. "Son, come here. I want to say something to you."

The young African got up slowly and walked to the old woman. She reached out her wrinkled hand and placed it on his shoulder.

"Do not be afraid of me. I know you have heard of me. All the children in this village have been warned to stay away from the old witch in the jungles. Ngonjo, you come here too. I want you to witness what I have to say."

The village chief moved quickly to the platform and stood beside Tene. Silence reigned as everyone waited to hear what the woman would say.

"From what I have heard from Ngonjo and from all of you today, I am going to tell you about something I did in my heart before I got up to speak."

Again she hesitated, catching her breath. Chief Paul sensed his mother was both nervous and tired.

"I asked Jesus to make my heart clean," she finally said. "I know He did or I would not be talking to you like this."

A cheer went up all over the little chapel. Becky Davis found herself clapping with the others.

"I have ways of finding out things. Tene," she said in her crackling voice, "my son, Ngonjo, uh—uh—Paul, has adopted you as his son. That makes me your grandmother and the highest village authority over you. I want you to go to that school to learn more about God. We all need to know more about Him. You can come back and teach us, my child."

The old woman then told how she had saved nearly every bit of money she had been able to earn from her gardening for the past years. She explained how it was buried in a number of glass jars near her hut in the forest. The people could hardly believe it.

"Some of that money is yours, Tene. It is to help you go to school and learn about God. It all belongs to God."

That night Paul and Becky talked into the early hours of the morning. The six-hour farewell service was something they would long remember.

"It's amazing!" said Becky. "The Lord had that money in an underground safe all the time, just waiting to help support Tene in Bible school."

"You're right," answered Paul, sleepily. "And to think that you and I never even heard of Chief Paul's mother until today. Chief Paul still doesn't know how she came into the service without him seeing her."

"The Lord sent her," said Becky. "It was His time for another miracle at Yanga."

8
A
Thief
Returns

Tene handed his new bicycle to Pastor Kondo who placed it gently on the ground. "There you are, Pastor," said the excited new Bible school student. "I really appreciate Mr. Davis bringing my baggage to school. I don't know how I could have done it."

"I knew they would do it for you," Pastor Kondo replied. "They are thrilled to see you go to Bible school. You are part of a wonderful miracle at Yanga, Tene."

The young African student snapped his fingers in his excitement. "And to think that Grandma Bio asked to come along so she could see where I would be studying."

"She sure has become your grandmother, all right," laughed Kondo. "Who would ever have thought that she had that much money hidden under the ground in those jars and bottles? When she knew you would be going into the villages on weekends to preach, she immediately thought of buying you a new bicycle. Then, too, it is really good thinking on her part not to pay all of your school expenses."

"You're right, Pastor," responded Tene. "She may be feeble in her body, but not in her thinking."

Just then Paul and Becky walked out of the nearby classroom building with Chief Paul's mother. The old lady gave a big, toothless grin, showing her delight in being able to come on the trip and visit the school.

"Tene will be happy here," she said in her crackling voice. "He will be a good student."

Kondo looked over at his young friend standing beside his baggage. "See what I mean, Tene? Grandma Bio is your main supporter in more ways than one. When you have someone like her to answer to, that alone should keep you faithful in your studies."

"After lunch we'll head back, Kondo," Paul Davis called as he helped Grandma Bio into the mission house. "You fellows had better come in. I think Mrs. Dykes has our meal ready for us."

Grandma Bio was all eyes as each one took his place at the table. This was her first time in a white man's home as well as her first experience in eating his strange foods. The Bible school director, Bill Dykes, prayed, and the food was passed around. Kondo, who had eaten many times in the Davis home, assisted the old lady with her meal. Everyone smiled when, during the meal, Grandma Bio reached over with her fork and gently tapped Tene on the hand for sticking the meat on his fork with his fingers.

"That was a delicious meal, Kathy," Becky said to the director's wife. "Thank you also for the lunch you packed for the road. Grandma Bio enjoyed her meal so much, I'm sure she'll be ready to try these sandwiches in an hour or two."

Tene hugged his grandmother, and she responded by blowing gently in each ear. "You don't often see that kind of affection anymore," Kondo said to Paul.

"It's different from our ways," Becky whispered to her husband, "but it's very precious to them."

The trip back to the mission station was uneventful. Only once was Paul concerned and that was when they had to cross a small log bridge which had been broken by a large cotton truck. Kondo walked ahead of the pickup, directing Paul across.

Their arrival in Yanga that evening was heralded by cheers from the villagers. Chief Paul was the first to greet them, and he helped his mother out of the cab. She was so excited and had so much to tell that Paul was fearful she might collapse from it all.

"Next time, you go," she said to her son. "You must see the school and eat that good food." A laugh went up from the crowd as she spoke.

It was late when Paul and Becky turned down the driveway to their house. It seemed strange that there should be people waiting for them at that time of night. They pulled up in front of the garage and stopped. Immediately they heard someone talking excitedly to Kondo, who had preferred to ride in the back of the truck where the air was cool.

"What is it, Kondo?" Paul asked as he stepped down from the cab.

"Someone broke into my house and stole my new bicycle while my wife was in the garden."

"Oh, no," said Becky, holding her hand to her face. "When did it happen?"

"Probably sometime this evening after it got dark and before she arrived home. She wanted to finish harvesting our peanuts, so she stayed in the garden until it got dark."

"But who would do such a thing to Kondo?" Becky questioned her husband after they were in the house. "He is so kind to everyone."

"I know he is, Honey. This leaves me puzzled. It's surely a comfort to know the Lord knows all about it. He knows where the bicycle is this very moment."

As the missionary couple prayed together before retiring for the night, Becky couldn't hold back the tears. "Lord," she prayed between sobs, "as Paul said, You know all about the theft of Kondo's bicycle. Please touch the heart of the one who took it and cause him to bring it back."

Sleep didn't come easily for the concerned couple. Becky tossed and turned long after her husband had gone to sleep.

The sound of the tam-tam startled Paul. It was unusual for him still to be in bed at six o'clock when Pele beat the drum.

"These late nights are getting to me," he whispered to himself. He quietly slipped from the bedroom so he wouldn't awaken Becky. As he unlocked the back door, he was surprised to see Pastor Kondo and several other men sitting around a small fire by the night guard's hut. Paul quickly stepped out into the yard and headed for the group.

"Good morning, Kondo. What brings you here so early in the morning?"

Pastor Kondo stood to greet his missionary friend. "Good morning, Mr. Davis. I have good news for you. My bicycle has been returned."

"Thank the Lord!" exclaimed Paul. "What happened?"

"Let me tell him," said the stranger standing next to Kondo.

"Mr. Davis," said the pastor, "this is Vol. Tell Mr. Davis what happened."

The short, stocky African began his story.

"I have watched Pastor Kondo with his new bicycle for many days now. I wanted a bicycle but had no money to buy one. So, I planned to steal his. Last night after dark and before his wife

45

returned home, I sneaked into the workmen's village and broke into his house. It was a bit of a problem to get out of the village without anyone seeing me, but I made it."

"But what made you bring it back?" questioned the missionary. "I really don't know," said the African. "I was riding along the dark road when all of a sudden a terrible fear came over me. I realized that I had stolen from a man of God and that the bicycle I was on belonged to God. I became so frightened I couldn't even pedal any longer. My legs just wouldn't work right. When I stopped, I was shaking all over."

"That is really something," said Paul, observing the young man. "Then what did you do?"

"I know this sounds strange, but I got down on my knees right there in the road and talked to God. I told Him I was sorry and that I would take the bicycle back to the pastor. I began to feel better immediately and walked the bicycle back to Pastor Kondo's house. I did not even want to ride it back because it did not belong to me and I was afraid of the pastor's God."

"Unbelievable," Paul whispered to himself.

"Pastor," said Vol, "you tell him the rest of the story."

"When I heard someone clapping his hands outside my house at two o'clock this morning, I went out to see who was calling me. There stood Vol with my bicycle. He told me what he just told you. I then talked to him about God's love for him and how Jesus died for his sins. God had already prepared his heart, Mr. Davis. He accepted Jesus right there in my front yard. I then took him in, gave him some food and a bed. We wanted you to be the first to hear what happened."

"Let's go and tell Mrs. Davis," said Paul, heading back toward the house. "She was greatly burdened for this matter, Kondo, and I want her to see and hear a testimony showing the power of our prayer-answering God."

"Amen," voiced Pastor Kondo as he followed with Vol. Becky Davis was about to see the answer to her prayer.

9

'Precious
in the
Sight
of the
Lord'

The missionary grapevine buzzed with the news about Tene. "I've never seen a young man apply himself as Tene has done this past semester," wrote Bill Dykes. "The village of Yanga can be proud of a student like him."

Ken and Marge Simms had just arrived at the Davis home and delivered the letter from Bill Dykes to Paul and Becky.

That's wonderful," responded Paul, pounding his fist into his hand. "Every letter we get from Bill and Kathy mentions Tene. He sure is serious about his studies."

"Say, Ken," Paul exclaimed, "here we are talking about Tene, and we haven't even asked you folks how you are doing. It is sure good to see you both again."

The doctor looked at Paul and then at Becky, who had dark circles under her eyes. "Well, when we received your last letter, I felt that Marge and I should visit you. A letter wouldn't have reached you before we got here, so we sent a telegram."

"Not again," laughed Becky, putting her arm around Marge. "Remember, this happened the last time you came."

"We thought about that," said Marge, "when we saw your surprised looks as we drove in. Ken said he felt like shouting 'SURPRISE' out the window when he saw your blank looks."

"Come on inside," interrupted Becky. "We don't have to stand and talk out here in the driveway."

Dr. Simms had not planned on such a soon return to the Yanga area, but after receiving a letter from the Davises that Becky had not been feeling well, he came immediately. The symptoms described in the communication gave the missionary doctor no small concern, and he thought it best to travel up country to examine Becky.

After the missionaries had enjoyed glasses of iced tea, Ken suggested that Becky have her examination. His heart sank as he discovered a rather large growth in the upper abdomen. Becky noticed the serious look on her co-worker's face.

"What do you find, Ken?" she asked in her soft voice. "Is there anything wrong?"

"I don't know what it is, Becky, but there is some kind of a mass in the upper abdomen. I think you and Paul should return to the capital city with us. I'd like to run some tests on you at the city's hospital."

The young missionary wife felt a strange sensation run through her body. Her eyes filled with tears as horrible thoughts flashed through her mind. Marge Simms, who was standing beside her bed, squeezed Becky's hand. The three left the bedroom and joined Paul, who was nervously sitting in the living room. He knew Becky wasn't well. More than once he had heard her groan with pain during the night. When he would say something to her, she always assured him that she would be all right. For some reason, deep inside him, Paul Davis knew his wife was seriously ill. He looked up as Becky entered the room. Her face was whiter than usual, causing the dark circles under her eyes to stand out even more.

"Paul," she said, "Ken wants us to go back with them to the capital city. He wants to run some tests on me at the hospital."

"When do you want to leave, Ken?" Paul asked, not too surprised at the doctor's decision.

"Since it's so late in the day, Paul, let's leave early tomorrow morning. That way, barring any car trouble, we can be in the city by tomorrow night."

The two couples sprang into action. Paul called Pastor Kondo and told him of their plans. Arrangements were made for the station's work projects to continue. A letter was sent to Chief Paul, informing him of the latest developments. Becky and Marge busied themselves packing several suitcases. Marge noticed that Becky packed as though she were leaving for good. She wondered what thoughts were going through her friend's mind.

"That's it, Marge," said Becky, showing the strain of the past three hours. "I think we have everything we'll need."

That night Becky slept very little. She lay for hours thinking of the past. She thought of her parents and how she had accepted Jesus as her Savior one night when, at the age of seven, she knelt beside her bed with her mother. She would never forget her high school days. It was then she had met Paul Davis. His spiritual stature and Christian testimony had caught her attention immediately. It wasn't until Bible college days though that she and Paul had begun to date. She thought of the school's annual missionary conference where, unknown to each other, they both responded to the invitation for missionary service. What a surprise it had been to look up and see Paul standing beside her. From that moment on, they knew that God had meant them for each other.

As morning approached, she thought of their marriage, acceptance by the mission board, deputation, language school, and finally, the field. Her heart jumped with excitement as she recalled the attack of Kota and his men, the conversion of Chief Ngonjo, Kota's conversion and death, the establishment of the work at Yanga, Tene's being called to Bible school and Bio's conversion.

Becky quietly took the handkerchief from under her pillow and wiped her eyes.

"Thank You, Father," she whispered, "for all these blessings. Thank You, too, for the privilege of being a part of them." The young missionary wife doubled up her knees to relieve the pain in her stomach. Finally, she drifted off to sleep.

"Honey, wake up."

Becky opened her eyes to see Paul standing beside her bed.

"I must have dozed off," she said, rubbing her eyes.

"I hope you more than dozed," said Paul, patting her on the head. "Come on, Honey. I hear Marge and Ken moving around."

The two couples had a quick breakfast and were soon in their pickups, ready to leave. Kondo had shared the news with the local Christians, and the long driveway was lined with men, women and children who had come to bid good-bye to their beloved missionaries. Pastor Kondo prayed before their departure. Becky's heart was again filled with praise to the Lord for the privilege of being a part of such a wonderful ministry. Many of the African Christians were closer to her than some members of her own family.

The trip to the city was made without difficulty. Becky was admitted to the hospital the next day, and tests were begun immediately. It was the morning of the third day that the doctor broke the news to his co-workers.

"You must leave immediately for the States. I'm booking you both on the next plane as medical evacuations in order to get the seats. I'll make the arrangements at the hospital in Atlanta for you."

Things happened so fast during the next two days that Paul and Becky hardly had time to think. Paul sent a telegram to Pastor Kondo, informing him of their return to America, and Kondo sent the word on to the village of Yanga. Chief Paul asked the local administrator to provide transportation for Kondo and himself to the capital city. When the two men walked into the hospital room, Paul and Becky couldn't believe their eyes.

"Kondo! Chief Paul!" Becky shouted with excitement in her voice. "It's so good to see you. When did you come? How did you get here? Where did—?"

"Hold on there, Honey," said Paul, smiling. "One question at a time."

Everyone laughed at Becky's outburst of questions. The men told their missionary friends how they had worked out the arrangements with the government administrator to come in his truck.

"That's great," said Paul. "You two are wonderful friends."

It was difficult for Paul and Becky to say good-bye. As the giant DC-8 raced down the runway, the heaviness upon their hearts and the lumps in their throats made it impossible for the missionary couple to even speak. Another chapter was being written in the lives of Paul and Becky Davis.

A week later Ken Simms pulled a cablegram envelope from the mailbox. His hands shook as he tore open the envelope. His eyes filled with tears as he read the message: "BECKY HOME WITH THE LORD. LETTER FOLLOWS."

Ken hurried to his car where Pastor Kondo and Chief Paul waited for him. The two men had not wanted to return home until they had heard something of their beloved missionaries. The doctor opened the door and slid into the seat. Somehow the men knew the news the blue and white envelope contained. After waiting some time to get his composure, Ken spoke to them.

"Our sister is with the Lord. I don't know what happened, but it must have been far worse than I suspected."

The two Africans bowed their heads and sat in silence. Tears rolled down their faces. Slowly Chief Paul looked up. His face was shining with tears. A smile appeared on his grief-stricken face.

"It makes God's house that much closer, Dr. Simms. Kota is there, and now Mrs. Davis. This is no mistake. The Lord was finished with her here and wanted her to be with Him."

"You're right, my brother," said Pastor Kondo. "God's Word says, 'Precious in the sight of the LORD is the death of his saints.' "

In his heart, Ken Simms praised God for his two African friends—the spiritual fruits of Paul and Becky Davis.

10

Bio's Request

The news of the death of Becky Davis left the village of Yanga in a state of shock. Little had they realized when their beloved missionaries left with Dr. and Mrs. Simms that within two weeks they would hear of Becky's Home-going. As the village Christians met each evening in the little chapel for a time of prayer, it became increasingly apparent that they missed their missionaries greatly.

In his prayer one evening, Chief Paul voiced the feelings of his people.

"Father, we confess that we do not understand Your ways many times. We do not want to question Your taking Mr. and Mrs. Davis from us, but we are human and we do miss them. Lord," he continued, "please send us a missionary. Kondo has his work at the workmen's village and Tene is still in school. Send someone to help us here at Yanga."

As the village chief ended his prayer, a drone of amens could be heard from the group of believers. Deep in his heart, Chief Paul believed that somehow God would answer their prayers.

Very early the following morning, the chief stirred on his bed. The cough was a soft one, but the village leader was sure he had heard it—or was he dreaming? No, there it was again. Someone was outside his hut and wanted to speak with him. The chief heard a rooster crow and knew that morning was approaching. He made his way to the door and opened it. To his surprise, there stood his mother with her tattered blanket thrown over her shoulders.

"Mama! What are you doing here so early? Come in. It's chilly out there."

The old lady entered her son's hut without saying a word. The village leader's wife had died three years before and he had not remarried. She made her way to the center of the large hut and sat down on the clay floor beside a smoldering fire.

"I have been doing some thinking during the night, Ngonjo, uh—uh—Paul."

The chief smiled. He knew his mother found it difficult to call him by any name other than the one she had given him at birth.

"I know I am not intelligent when it comes to writing or reading, but I do believe God gave me a clear mind."

There was no doubt about Bio's ability to think clearly. Her weakened physical condition did not seem to have any effect on her mind.

"What have you been thinking about, Mama?" her son asked as he made some coffee.

"Well, it may seem as if I am out of my mind for saying this, but I believe you should go to the capital city and ask Dr. and Mrs. Simms to come and live in this area. They know us and have been a big part of the work of God here. In fact, Paul, as the oldest member of this village, and as your mother, I'm asking you to do this for us."

The village leader was stunned at what he had heard. The interest of his mother in the Lord's work was an unbelievable change. She had changed from one who had worshiped Satan only a few months earlier to one who now served and honored God. It was a change to behold.

"Maybe they will not come, Mama. You know, they have their work in the capital city."

"They will come, my son, even if you have to take me down there to get them. I have talked to the Lord about this enough to know that this is what He wants us to do."

The chief could not help but chuckle to himself at the confidence of his mother.

"When you talk like that, Mama, I know there is only one thing for me to do, and that is to go and see Dr. and Mrs. Simms."

At the very moment Chief Paul and his mother were discussing the idea of the Simms' coming to Yanga, God was working in the hearts of that missionary couple in the capital city.

"I can't get the village of Yanga off my mind," Ken said that morning after he had returned from seeing one of the Christians in the nearby government hospital. "Ever since I had the privilege of leading Chief Paul to the Lord, I've had a heavy burden for that work."

"I do, too, Ken," responded Marge. "Paul will probably not

return to the field for quite a while, if he does come back, and the need for missionaries in that region is so great."

"If there were no hospital here, it might be different," Ken said. "But the people here can receive medical care. Up in that part of the country, there is no medical help anywhere."

"What would it take to show us, Ken?" Marge asked with a serious look in her eyes.

"I don't think it would take much, Honey. I'm sure we are ready to go right now. Let's wait a few more days to see if there is any direction from the Lord other than the burden He has placed on our hearts."

Back up-country, Pastor Kondo had heard that the government administrator was planning a trip to the capital city. He immediately sent word to Chief Paul. Just the day before the African chief had told him about his desire to go to the capital to speak with Dr. and Mrs. Simms. Kondo was overwhelmed with the thought of having a missionary couple come and live among them again. Chief Paul sent word that two places were to be reserved in the government truck—one for himself and one for the pastor. Hearing of the chief's request, the administrator sent his chauffeur to pick up the two men.

As Chief Paul climbed into the cab, his mother stood nearby. "This is God working, my son. He put the idea into the administrator's heart to go to the capital city at this time. He is always right in everything He does."

The truck made the trip in two days. The government official stopped in the villages along the way to visit with the chiefs and to inquire how the peanut gardens were progressing. Chief Paul and Pastor Kondo had many opportunities to witness among the villagers, and a number of them accepted Christ.

It was raining when the truck pulled up in front of the mission station house in the capital city. Marge Simms heard the voices outside and hurried to the window to see who was coming.

"Ken! It's Chief Paul and Pastor Kondo!"

Ken, who had been busy preparing for his Sunday messages, emerged quickly from his study. "Chief Paul! Pastor Kondo! I wonder why they've come to the city."

The missionary couple opened the door and stepped onto the front porch. The rain on the aluminum roof made it difficult for them to hear the chief's words as he called to them. Ken ran out to the cab and shook hands with the administrator, thanking him for bringing the two men. Chief Paul and Pastor Kondo also shook hands with him and mentioned that they would contact him about the return trip. As the truck departed, the three men made their way into the house.

"How are you, Chief Paul?" Ken asked as he took the village leader's coat.

"I'm fine, thank you, Dr. Simms. And how are you people?" The three men engaged in conversation as Marge served some coffee and cookies.

"If you don't mind my asking you, Chief, what brings you and Kondo to the city?"

"I was afraid you would never ask us, Dr. Simms," answered the tall African. "You brought us to the city."

"I—I don't understand," stammered Ken. "What do you mean?"

"Pastor Kondo and I have come to ask you to be our missionaries. I know you have a mission station near the government center, and for you to live there is all right with us. We just want you in our area where you can be part of the work at Yanga."

"Chief Paul," said Ken, reaching over to take Marge's hand, "we believe you are the Lord's answer. He has burdened our hearts for that area, and we've been simply waiting upon Him to show us what to do. He has just done that."

The chief then told the missionaries how his mother had come to talk with him. He mentioned how she was so sure that this was God's will that, if need be, she'd come to the city herself and speak with them.

"Bless her heart," said Marge, moved by the story. "It will be wonderful living near you all."

"We will call the mission station Yanga Two, if that's all right with you people and Pastor Kondo," spoke the chief.

"That's fine with me," answered Kondo, filled with excitement at the thought of having a missionary couple again.

"Yanga Two," repeated Ken to himself. "That sounds so good." He looked at Marge, her face wet with tears of joy. "Honey, we'll notify the mission field council immediately of our desire to move. I'm sure they'll be glad to hear of our decision. Ever since Paul and Becky left, we've all been praying that God would send someone else there—and to think, He's sending us."

Chief Paul and Pastor Kondo quietly sat by, listening and thanking God in their hearts.

11

A
Strange
Visitor

The large palm leaf arch over the entrance of the driveway caught the eyes of Ken and Marge Simms as they approached the mission station, Yanga Two. Bright red bougainvillea dotted the green arch, giving it just the right color and attraction.

"It's beautiful!" Marge exclaimed when she saw it. "How thoughtful of them to do this for us."

As the blue pickup turned into the drive, the missionary couple could hardly believe their eyes. The one hundred yards to the house were lined with beautiful tropical flowers. Hundreds of Africans stood in the yard waiting for their arrival.

"I've never seen anything like this," Ken said in a choked voice.

"And to think," added Marge, "they have done this for us."

The reception of hugs, kisses and handshakes that followed was beyond anything the Simms had ever experienced. One villager after another stepped up to welcome the doctor and his wife. Many of the older Africans gently blew into the ears of the white couple. When the Simms thought it was over, the people began to present their gifts. Never before had they been showered with so many things. The gifts included chicken eggs, rice, peanuts, goats, bananas, pineapples, fish and even a case of orange soft drink that someone had brought in from the capital city for the special occasion.

"Why have you done so much for us?" Marge asked, shaking Pastor Kondo's hand.

"Because we love you. This is the way our people show their love. When you love someone, you give him gifts."

Some of the women of the village had thoroughly cleaned the

house, leaving it spotless. The beds were made with clean, new linens. Several new kerosene lamps were placed about the house.

"Where did all this come from, Chief Paul?" Ken asked, pointing to the bed linens.

"We sent two men to the capital city for them. We wanted them to be a surprise for you."

"Oh, it is, Chief Paul," exclaimed Marge. "You dear people really surprised us. You make us feel right at home."

"You are home," responded a cracky voice. "We are your people and you are our missionaries."

Marge looked up to see a little old African woman standing in the doorway.

"Dr. and Mrs. Simms," spoke out Chief Paul, "this is my mother. Please forgive me for being a little slow to introduce her, but I did not know she would be able to come to this welcoming."

"Although we've never met," Marge said, turning to Bio and taking her hand, "I think I would know you anywhere. We've heard so much about you. But I, too, am surprised to see you here. Tell me, how did you get here from Yanga One? It's such a long way."

"I rode on the back of a bicycle. Ever since I bought that bicycle for Tene, all the young people want one. Of course, they work hard to earn their money to buy them. There must be four or five of them in the village now."

Ken and Marge looked at each other and smiled, thinking of the old African woman riding the twenty miles on a bicycle.

After the Africans unpacked the truck and carried the missionaries' baggage into the house, Chief Paul asked everyone to go back outside for the reception service. The large crowd was quiet and orderly. Pastor Kondo stood behind a small table to act as the master of ceremonies. The families from the workmen's village began the service by quoting Bible verses and singing a hymn. The Christians from Yanga One, led by their chief, then quoted a number of verses and also sang. Bio was asked to give her testimony. She told how she was bound by fear of superstition and witchcraft for many years. The people laughed as she acted out how she chased her son, Paul, away from her house after he informed her that he had accepted Christ as his Savior. Few could hold back the tears as she referred to her wasted life and how she now wanted every moment of her sunset years to count for Jesus. A number of others gave their testimonies or sang in small groups. Finally Pastor Kondo asked Chief Paul to speak.

"Friends," he said, looking out over the crowd, "today we witness another answer to prayer. I have invited a number of my fellow chiefs to come today so they can hear firsthand what God has done and continues to do among us."

He stopped, bowed his head a moment and then continued. "We cannot have such a service without mentioning our dear brother and sister, Mr. and Mrs. Davis. Our sister is with the Lord today, but her spiritual fruit continues to multiply among us. Only when we get to God's house will we know the results of their ministry. We miss them both more than our tongues can tell. Now God, in His perfect way, has sent us Dr. and Mrs. Simms. We love them, too, just as we loved Mr. and Mrs. Davis."

The next two weeks were exciting ones for Ken and Marge. People they had never met came to welcome the new white couple. Before they realized it, a month had passed. Then Martin Blanc appeared on the scene. Ken first noticed the stranger in a Sunday morning service.

"I'm glad to meet you," he told the visitor as he left the church that day. "Come back again."

"Oh, I will," responded Martin. "These are my people, and I expect to be around here awhile."

As Ken and Marge walked from the church to their home, they talked about the new visitor. "There's something about that man that puzzles me," said Ken. "He seems friendly enough, but I have a reservation about him which I can't explain."

"Did you notice how he walked with a limp?" Marge asked, mounting the front veranda of their mission home.

"Yes, I did. It looked as if he had a thick bandage wrapped around his leg just above his ankle."

Marge went into the kitchen to take a look at the antelope roast she had in the oven. Ken followed to continue their conversation. "He said he expected to be around here awhile, and these are his people. I wonder what he meant?"

"I don't know, Ken, but I have a feeling we're going to see plenty of Mr. Blanc before too long."

Marge carefully slid the roast from the oven and placed it on the back of the wood stove. The hind leg had been one of the many gifts given to the Simms upon their arrival at Yanga Two. How thankful they were for the way God had led them to the Banda tribe—a tribe that was also the target of a satanic plan!

12

The Union

Early the next morning, as Ken walked through the yard to his workmen's class, he met Kondo standing beside the garage. The African seemed a bit cool to the missionary doctor.

"Good morning, Kondo," Ken greeted his friend. "How are you today?"

"I'm fine," answered the pastor. "I've come to ask you to treat Martin Blanc. I have told him about the apartment you have here for patients, and he wants to move in today."

Kondo's bold approach took Ken by surprise. He wanted to ask his friend if there was something wrong, but, on second thought, he decided not to say anything.

"Well, it's empty right now, Kondo. I see no reason why he can't come, but maybe I should examine his leg first. Perhaps it's not serious enough to confine him to the apartment."

"It is bad enough, Dr. Simms," the pastor told him. "Since you have the truck, you can go pick him up this morning. He does not want to walk on his leg."

"But he was in church yesterday, Kondo," said Ken, somewhat puzzled by the attitude of the pastor. "He limped some, but his leg didn't seem to be causing him any great pain."

"I will go with you, Dr. Simms. He has two wives with him, so it will be a load for your truck when they get all their baggage in it." Ken felt sick as he later described Kondo's attitude to Marge. "He practically ordered me to go get Mr. Blanc this morning. That's not like Kondo. There's something wrong with this whole thing."

As Ken drove out of the mission station, he noticed the concerned look on his wife's face. Marge also sensed that things weren't right. Ken was sure she was not mistaken about Martin

Blanc. Already he could see the bad influence the stranger had on Pastor Kondo.

Martin's wives had their baggage ready when Ken arrived. There was no doubt in their minds that the missionary would come at Kondo's request. They quickly loaded the pickup with the bags of peanuts, rice, manioc, dried fish, several mattresses, suitcases, a bicycle and cooking pots and pans. Martin and Kondo climbed into the front seat with Ken. The trip back to the station was embarrassing to Ken as the two men spoke to each other in the Arabic language. The missionary was convinced they were discussing matters about which they didn't want him to be aware.

"This is just the right size for us, Dr. Simms," Martin said as he stretched out on the chaise lounge which one of his wives unfolded for him.

"I'm glad you like it, Mr. Blanc. Would you mind if I looked at your leg?"

As Ken examined the ulcered leg, he had the strange feeling that his patient was laughing at him. But then, maybe he was just imagining things. After all, people do have bad days. Maybe this was one of those days.

"With some good treatment, Mr. Blanc, your leg should be well on the mend in a week.. The ulcer isn't too deep, so it shouldn't leave a big scar."

"Thank you, Dr. Simms," Martin called as Ken headed for his house. "I'm not sure I want to leave this place in a week."

As the days passed, Ken saw a marked improvement in Martin's leg. The thing that concerned the doctor and his wife the most, however, was the continual stream of Africans—Christians and non-Christians—who made their way to the patient's apartment. The missionary couple noticed a definite lack of friendliness among their African believers. The week passed without any indication on the part of Martin or his wives that they were planning to move out. At the end of the second week, Ken spoke to Martin about moving in order to make room for other patients.

"You can see that I'm still not well, doctor," Martin said sarcastically. "When I feel well enough to walk, I'll let you know."

Ken was heavily burdened with the problem of Martin Blanc. He felt as if his hands were tied. Never before had he been so frustrated. All the love he showed to his patient seemed to be taken for granted. Pastor Kondo was also the object of concern. His messages for the past few Sundays had definitely been different. He was spending a lot of time with Martin Blanc, and even became disturbed when Ken went near the two of them.

Ken and Marge sat in the little grass-covered building one afternoon as Kondo closed the midweek prayer meeting. Instead of giving his usual farewell to the believers, Kondo surprised the missionaries by saying, "Good-bye, my comrades." As he spoke, he raised his fist and held it high. The sound of the word struck like a bolt of lightning!

"Where did he learn that?" Marge whispered, her voice showing deep emotion.

"I don't know, Honey, but it doesn't sound good. I'm going to speak with Kondo about this."

"Why are you so concerned about the word *comrade,* Dr. Simms?" questioned Kondo when he was approached that same evening. "And what is wrong with raising my fist? You wave your hand. Well, I've learned that *comrade* is used in the free countries of the world. And the fist, that means power—conquering power."

"Where did you learn these things, Kondo?" asked the bewildered missionary.

"From Martin Blanc. He is here to give our people many things. You see, Dr. Simms, you are a foreigner. You have your own country, so you are not really interested in us. Oh, you may say you are, but we know you are not. You have never told us about the union."

"About what?" asked Ken, surprised at what Kondo had said.

"The union," repeated the pastor. "Martin is organizing a union among us. All of us are contributing to it. I have already given him my money."

"What does it do for you?" questioned Ken.

"It will provide transportation—trucks to haul our crops to market. We will also have buses to provide transportation for our people. Martin is going to get us big machines to work our gardens. Our homes are going to have electric lights, and we will pump the water from our wells by just pushing a button. We will be able to pay doctors to come and live among us. All of our people will have shoes and clothing. We are poor people, Dr. Simms, but Martin is going to make us all rich with the union."

"Kondo! What has happened to you? You aren't the same man I saw that night when the men from Yanga One attacked the mission house! Remember how you risked your life to protect Mr. and Mrs. Davis?"

Pastor Kondo ignored Ken's direct questions. "You foreigners are all alike, Dr. Simms. You have your trucks, good food, nice homes and beautiful clothes. We want to have them too! Martin Blanc is here now. He came all the way from Moscow where he trained to help poor people—people like us who need that kind of help."

"Kondo, do you know where Moscow is located?"

"All I know is what Martin said. He told us that it is a big city where a lot of nice white people live. He said they are the kind of white people who want to help the poor. Your country does not like poor people, Dr. Simms. Martin says your country is run by imperialists."

Marge, who had quietly stood by listening to the conversation, was shocked by the pastor's words. Only a miracle of the Lord could save His work among the Banda tribe. Martin Blanc's influence among the believers was devastating, and it seemed that on every side he had gained the upper hand. Ken felt as if he couldn't listen any more, but there was one other question he had to ask Kondo before he and Marge went to their house.

"Does Chief Paul know about Martin Blanc?"

"Of course, he does," answered the pastor. "He has visited Martin at least three times since he has lived here in the apartment."

"He has?" exclaimed Ken. "Why didn't he stop in to say hello to us? He never comes near Yanga Two but what he stops in to see us."

"Let me say he used to stop in to see you, Dr. Simms," replied Kondo. "Martin told him that he would not provide one piece of equipment for Yanga One if he continued his friendship with you. In fact, Chief Paul has already promised next year's cotton crop to the union."

"But when did all of this take place?" asked Ken.

"At night, Dr. Simms, while you were sleeping. Chief Paul was brought by bicycle to the apartment and then left before morning. You see, Dr. Simms, Martin is well organized. He is intelligent."

As the missionary couple sadly made their way to their house, it was difficult for them to believe that one man could do so much damage in such a little time. Ken already knew his next move. He would leave in the morning for Yanga One.

13

Accusations

The next morning as Ken walked into the workmen's Bible class, about half of the men were missing.

"Where is everyone?" Ken asked, looking around the group.

"They quit, Dr. Simms. They will come on payday to get their money, but they are through working for you. They say you are a capitalist."

"A capitalist!" repeated the missionary. "Where have you heard that word?"

"People have been using it for about two months now. When they talk about you and Mrs. Simms, they never call you missionaries anymore. You are called capitalists."

"Do you know what the word means, John?" Ken asked.

"It means rich people like you. The talk is that Americans are spies. They go to foreign countries as government workers and missionaries to spy and rob."

"Do you believe that?" Ken began to feel sick deep in his stomach.

"My heart does not want to believe it, Dr. Simms, but Martin's words keep filling my head, telling me it is true."

The missionary doctor felt sorry for John and the others. He knew they were victims of a vicious satanic attack through one who called himself a Christian, but who was putting his Marxist training into practice.

At breakfast, Ken told Marge about the missing workmen.

"But they didn't even give you any notice, Ken!" Marge exclaimed.

"I know that, Honey. The Lord knows all about it and we must trust Him. He's greater than all the forces of Satan."

The road to Yanga One seemed longer than usual. Ken thought it best for Marge to stay home. He had assured her there would be no danger in his going alone. A nervous chill ran through him, though, as the village came into view. As usual, he drove in and parked under a flamboyant tree. Several children ran to greet him.

"Hello, Dr. Simms," they shouted, waiting for Ken to step down from the cab. "You have been away from us a long time," said one of the older children.

"I sure have," answered the doctor. "Where's Chief Paul? Is he around?"

Before the children could answer, Ken heard the familiar voice call out from the large hut in the center of the village. "I'll be right there, Dr. Simms. Wait there by your truck."

Although he had started for the chief's house, Ken stopped and returned to the pickup. Shortly, the chief made his appearance from the hut and walked toward Ken.

"I want to thank you for coming, Dr. Simms, but I find it hard to say it. You see, I have something on my heart that I must tell you."

As the village chief spoke, Ken could see the absence of the joy that once shone on the leader's face.

"You brought us God's Word, but you did it as a cover. I have heard from a reliable source that you American missionaries are really here to spy on our land. You report to your colonial government which, in turn, uses the information to make things harder for us. I am surprised at you, Dr. Simms. We really thought you people were our true friends."

"We are your true friends, Chief Paul," Ken replied. The familiar sick feeling began to sweep over him. "We've done only things to help you. We love you people. God sent us to you."

"It sounds good, Dr. Simms, but that is about all. We are going to set up a diesel generator here in the village. There will be no more kerosene lamps. My people will have electric lights. The women will not have to pull the water from the well with ropes anymore. We are just going to push a button and the water will come to us in pipes. You are only one doctor, but the union will bring us many. They will be white like you, but they come from a country that loves poor people like us."

The chief pointed to the missionary's truck. "We are going to have our own village truck. And there will be buses to carry our people from one village to another. It will be free transportation too."

"Who is—?"

"I do not want to hear any more, Dr. Simms. You have been

good to us, but that was only to gather information from us. And to think we trusted you like a brother."

Again Chief Paul pointed to the truck. "Please get in now, Dr. Simms, and leave us alone. If I were you, I would pack up and go back to America."

Ken could not hold back the tears as he drove to the mission station. It all seemed like a terrible nightmare to him.

"Lord," he prayed aloud, "please stop this attack by Satan on these people. Father, send someone to us who will stand with us. Someone, Lord, who can expose Martin Blanc's evil doings."

After their noon meal, Ken and Marge sat in the living room going over the morning events at Yanga One. A knock at the door interrupted their conversation. Ken was surprised to find Martin Blanc standing on the veranda waiting for him.

"Hello, Martin," the doctor said in his usual kind voice. "How is your leg?"

"That is what I came to tell you, Dr. Simms. My leg is good enough to walk on now, and we will be moving this afternoon. If you will be kind enough to offer the services of your truck, you can take us back to the government post. My cousin lives there and he is going to give me the use of his house."

The Simms were overwhelmed with joy to know that they were soon to lose their unwelcome guest. "That's the best news we've heard in a long time," Ken said as he emptied a jerry can of gas into the truck.

"It's good news, Honey," replied Marge, "but we still have the problem of his influence on these people. I'm glad, though, that he won't be living here in our medical apartment anymore."

Martin's wives loaded the pickup truck as he stood by, talking with Ken. The missionary was surprised at the friendly attitude of the African.

"Probably none of my people have told you, Dr. Simms, why I have a French name."

"No, no one has, Martin," answered the doctor. "I knew it wasn't an African name and thought perhaps you chose it yourself."

"My father is French. He was a colonial government officer. My mother is Banda. That is how I can claim these people as my people and, at the same time, I am a French citizen. I had all my schooling in France."

Ken wanted to ask him about Moscow and his training there,

but decided that perhaps it wouldn't be the wise thing to do at that point.

As soon as the truck was loaded, Ken left the station. When he arrived at the government post, a large crowd was on hand to unload the truck for Martin. Everything seemed to be well planned, which proved to the missionary that he was dealing with a very clever man. As Ken started the truck's motor to return to the station, some of the crowd jeered at him. Martin walked up to the driver's side of the cab.

"Good-bye, Dr. Simms. You have a very useful truck. It could do a lot of hauling for our community."

"Good-bye, Martin," Ken said, finding it difficult to smile.

That night, Ken and Marge went over the day's events, starting again with Ken's visit to Yanga One. Sadness was evident in their voices as they talked of the reversal of the attitude among the area's believers.

"Today when I was coming back from Yanga One," Ken said, "I asked the Lord to send us someone to help us. I prayed that God would stop this satanic attack on these people."

"But who is there, Ken?" questioned Marge, with a puzzled look on her pretty face.

"I don't know, Honey, but the Lord can raise up someone. It seems as if everyone is against us."

That night, the troubled couple went to bed with heavy hearts. As Marge prayed, she thanked the Lord again for His Word and the promises in it for them. Ken lay on his back, looking up into the darkness of the room. He knew that Marge, too, was finding it difficult to go to sleep. Finally he spoke to his wife.

"Listen to this verse, Honey. The Lord just gave it to me. First Peter 5:7, 'Casting all your care upon him; for he careth for you.' "

The verse was just what they both needed. Within a short time they had drifted off to sleep, unaware of the dark figure slowly making its way along the side of the house to their bedroom window.

14
The
Midnight
Visitor

"**K**en! Wake up!" Marge Simms whispered, shaking her husband. "Ken! Someone's at the window. Wake up!"

Ken sat straight up in bed. For a moment, he couldn't remember where he was. Then he heard his wife's voice and felt her hand on his arm.

"Someone's at the window, Ken. I heard him scratching the screen."

The doctor quickly slipped out of bed and, in spite of the danger of scorpions and centipedes, walked to the window in his bare feet. He pushed his face up against the screen to get a better look outside. He jumped back, though, when a dark figure raised up before him.

"Who are you?" Ken demanded nervously. As he stepped back from the window, the person pushed closer until a head was against the screen.

"You need not be afraid," came the familiar voice. "I have come to talk to you."

"Bio!" Ken exclaimed, surprised at hearing his own voice. "What are you doing here?"

"Shhh!" she whispered with her finger to her lips. "No one must hear us. I have come to talk with you." The couple hurried to the front room where Ken opened the door for the chief's mother. She entered quickly.

"Let's sit down," said Marge. "You sound as if you're out of breath, Bio."

"I am a bit tired," responded the old woman. "I have been walking since this morning to get here."

"But why didn't you send word to me?" asked Ken. "I would have come to get you."

"Oh, no, Dr. Simms," said Bio, shaking her head. "Not one person in our tribe must know I am here with you."

"But how did you get here?" Marge asked. "Surely people saw you walking on the road."

"That is just it," answered Bio. "I did not walk on the road. I traveled through the jungle. I grew up in that jungle as a little girl, and I know it as I know the inside of my own hut."

"Let me get you something to eat, Bio," said Marge, getting up from her chair. "You and Dr. Simms talk. I'll get the food ready."

"Thank you, Mrs. Simms. I will not turn down your offer. I am hungry and I have to get back into the jungle before daylight. That will get me back home tomorrow afternoon."

Ken found it difficult to imagine how this frail little old woman sitting before him could have traveled all those miles through the jungle to get to them.

"What is it that you want to see us about, Bio?"

"It's about that man, Martin Blanc. I knew him when he was born. His mother and I knew each other when we were small girls."

The old woman stopped to catch her breath. "He is a bad man, Dr. Simms. He has come here to deceive his own people. That is why he has spread so many lies about you and your country. His mother is dead now, and even though he never says it publicly, she gave him to me when she was dying."

"You mean, you are—"

"I am his recognized mother. There are only two people alive who know this—Martin and I. The relationship cannot be broken, because his mother established it, even though she was dying. He may not like it, but he will not go against her decision."

"Does Chief Paul have any idea about this?" questioned Ken.

"No one knows about it. It is something one does not talk about. I know it and Martin knows it. I also know that he has a French wife. You wouldn't think it, seeing him traveling around the countryside with those two Banda women."

"Has he seen you since he's been here?"

"No, because I have deliberately kept out of his way."

Marge entered with some sandwiches and coffee. Ken prayed, thanking the Lord for the food. The old lady ate as if she were starving. Finally, she settled back in the chair to finish what she had started to say before eating.

"I want you to forget about returning to your own country," she said, shaking her finger at Ken. "Martin believes he can scare you out of here. He knows that you, as a foreigner, can see through his promises. My people are blind when it comes to seeing him as a deceiver. He knows that because he is one of them."

"You speak with great wisdom, Bio," said the missionary.

"What wisdom I have, Dr. Simms, the Lord gave to me. He is the One Who put it in my heart to come and talk with you and Mrs. Simms." As Bio spoke, Ken realized that the answer to his prayer that morning in the truck was already on its way before he even prayed. A wave of excitement rippled through his body as he thought of how God was beginning to work in their behalf.

"Remember what I said. You people stay right here," commanded the chief's mother. "I know I am an old woman, but I believe God can use me to bring a stop to all of this which Martin is doing. My son, Paul, has placed his confidence in Martin. The only thing that will break it is for him to see Martin Blanc as he actually is—a thief and a liar."

Marge shivered as she listened to Bio's strong words. It made her feel good to hear the tone of authority in the crackling voice. She smiled as she looked at the little figure before her. Who would have thought that God would send them a woman, and especially one of the oldest women in the tribe, to stand up against the Communist-trained agent?

Bio stood to go. "I must be careful when I leave. I do not want Martin or his wives to see me. I have been told they are living here."

"They're not here anymore, Bio," said Ken. "Martin came and asked me to take him back to the post this afternoon. I don't know why he left, but we're glad he did."

"God moved him out, my friends," snickered the old woman with her toothless grin. "I did not know the Lord was going to do it that fast, but I asked Him to get that man off your mission station."

Ken and Marge continued to be amazed at the simple faith of the chief's mother. They were sad to see their friend disappear into the darkness from which she had come.

"She's a marvel, Ken," Marge whispered. "For an old woman in her condition, she sure is courageous to do what she's doing. Why, I don't think I could make it through the jungle even in the daytime, and here she is traveling through it in pitch darkness."

Ken and Marge talked until almost morning. For some reason, they felt the end of Martin Blanc's activities among the Banda tribe was now in sight.

15

Kondo
Returns

Three days after Bio's secret visit to Yanga Two, a runner arrived at Martin Blanc's headquarters. The educated African quickly opened the envelope and read the note containing Chief Paul's signature.

> I hear you have left the mission station and are now living at the post. Your leg must be healed well enough for you to travel. Therefore, I want you to come to Yanga One this Sunday. You will have the entire morning service to explain to my people how and when they will receive the many things you have promised them. They are anxious to hear of your plans. I am inviting our neighboring chiefs and their people to come hear you. There may be a thousand people here waiting for you when you arrive on Saturday. I expect you to stay overnight with us on Saturday and Sunday.

The French-African looked at the runner. "Has your chief invited the people from the other villages yet?"

"Yes, he has, sir. The other runners left when I did. They have all received the word by now. We are all anxious to hear you. The people in Yanga One have already begun construction on a garage for the truck that our village will receive. Chief Paul has also said that every house will have electric lights. Yes, sir, we are all excited about the whole thing. You surely are intelligent to get us so many things with such a small amount of money. As you told us before, the missionaries could never do that."

Martin seemed a bit nervous as he took a pen and scribbled off a note for the runner to take back to his chief. The pressure was beginning to build, and he wondered how he could stall much longer.

Meanwhile, back at Yanga Two, Ken and Marge were beginning to see signs of a breakthrough. Pastor Kondo, who had supported Martin Blanc, was asking questions of the missionaries.

"Tell me about this country, Russia," he asked Ken one day after class. "Are there a lot of churches there like you have in your country?"

The missionary explained how Russia was a Communist country and that communism is anti-God. He told how the true Christians in Russia are persecuted by the government and worship in underground churches.

"But he talks about a union and what it can do for us here if we contribute to it," said Kondo.

"I don't want to falsely accuse Mr. Blanc," Ken said, "but the union name I've heard mentioned is the largest Communist-controlled union in France. I believe your friend, Martin Blanc, is a tool of the Communists and has been sent here to Africa to plant the seeds of communism. Of course, the best place for them to send him to work is among his own people."

"Why didn't I see all this before, Dr. Simms?"

"Mainly because Martin is very clever. He didn't attack your faith. He simply started by trying to get rid of the ones who brought you the Word of God. He even started to meet with us as soon as he arrived. You see, Kondo, Martin is well trained. He knows what he can do as well as those things he can't do, at least for now. Once he got rid of the missionaries, then he would slowly introduce things to undermine your faith in God's Word. He would do it so cleverly that most of the Christians wouldn't realize it was happening. That's the way Satan works."

"One thing he used was to point out that he is one of you whereas we are foreigners. That speaks loudly to some people, Kondo. All he had to do was to get a few people to support him, and then the whole thing grew. The African people are close-knit, and family ties run deep. A few key family members gave him the start he needed, and he knew it."

"Dr. Simms," spoke the African pastor, "I'm asking you to forgive me for the way I have treated you. I can't imagine how I was so easily fooled by what Martin had to say."

"You don't know how good it is to hear you talk like this, Kondo," replied Ken, fighting to keep back the tears. "Our hearts have been broken over this whole affair, because we know what a farce this union is. We do forgive you, our brother. We have no ill feelings toward you or any of the Banda people."

The two men bowed their heads and prayed together. Pastor Kondo confessed to the Lord his rebellious spirit and the unkind things he had said to his missionary co-workers. After they finished praying, the two shook hands and embraced each other.

"This is better," said the pastor, smiling. "Once again I have the peace of the Lord in my heart. How easy it is to slip and get out of fellowship with Him."

"You're right, Kondo," replied Ken. "Oh, by the way, Kondo, I don't think I would use the word *comrade* anymore if I were you. You see, it's a Communist term."

"Thank you, Dr. Simms. I'm thankful to the Lord that you didn't leave when we asked you to, but rather stayed on with us."

"That's because God called me and sent me here, Kondo. If we were here on our own, we would have left defeated and broken-hearted. But this is His work, not man's."

"What should I do now, Dr. Simms, to stop this movement among us?"

Ken thought for a few moments and then spoke. "Preach the Word of God, Kondo. Stay in the Word and God will do the rest. I believe the time will come when you will want to mention the union and Martin Blanc by name, but right now, just preach God's Word. You will have opportunity to speak to people about Mr. Blanc's activities, but I don't think it would be wise to make that the main theme of your messages from the pulpit. God will give you direction and wisdom in handling this matter."

"Thank you again, Dr. Simms. I noticed that you and Mrs. Simms have been rather quiet throughout this whole thing. You have shown love and patience to us who have been caught up in it. God has given you great wisdom."

"Thank you, Kondo. I'm thrilled that you have seen the sinfulness of this terrible movement. You are a wonderful encouragement to us. Once again, we have seen God answer prayer. Satan is not going to destroy this work here among the Banda tribesmen. It's amazing how God, in His own perfect way, brings about the right decisions at just the right times."

"Kondo," said Ken, placing his hand on the pastor's shoulder, "Stand fast and watch God give us the victory. The battle is not ours, but the Lord's."

As the African pastor returned to the village, once again his heart was filled with praises to his God.

"Father," he prayed as he walked along, "how could I have done this to You? Thank You for bringing me back into fellowship with You and help me, Lord, not to stray away again."

Back at Yanga One, Bio was busy putting together her own plans for Martin's arrival. Since her conversion, her son, Chief Paul, had seen to it that she lived in the village with the rest of the people. He built her a new hut right beside his own, which was located in the center of the village. When Tene went to Bible school, Bio had revealed the large sum of money she had hidden in sealed jars under the ground near her hut in the jungle. But she never revealed the other half of her underground safe just a few yards away. Little by little, she was able to transfer it to her hut in the village without being detected. There she buried it in the floor. That was the safest place in the event that fire destroyed her hut. In fact, for many of the older Africans, hiding their wealth in the ground was a common practice.

Slowly Bio lifted the glass jar from the hole in the floor. She took off the lid and pulled out the piece of paper from inside. The paper was a letter, and the handwriting was that of Martin Blanc!

16

My One
Little
Son

The next few days saw a wonderful change take place in the workmen's village. A small group of believers began to meet each evening for prayer for the Lord's work. High on the list of prayer requests was the village of Yanga One and Chief Paul. The news had spread that Martin Blanc was going to meet with the people on Sunday morning, and this was also a matter of prayer for the Christians.

Saturday afternoon Martin arrived in Yanga One, and Bio made sure she was out of the village when he arrived.

"Hello, Chief Paul," Martin said, getting off his bicycle. "How is my good comrade today?"

"Everything is fine here at Yanga One," answered the village leader. "I hear things are not the same at Yanga Two. Have you heard any news from there, Martin?"

The visitor appeared surprised at the chief's remarks. "No, I have not heard anything. What have you heard?"

"That Pastor Kondo has changed his heart. They tell me he is friendly with the missionaries again, and even leads a nightly prayer meeting, praying for all of us who have agreed to be helped by you. I do not understand his turning his back on all those good things we are going to get from the union."

Martin was unusually quiet in his response to the chief. He was not prepared for such pressure from the Banda people.

"Well, it takes time for any program to develop, and maybe Pastor Kondo is not patient enough to wait for this to happen," Martin said. "After all, something big like this does not happen overnight. I almost forgot to ask you, Chief Paul," said the visitor, changing the subject, "how is your cotton planting coming?"

Early the next morning the people began to arrive from the nearby villages. By eight o'clock the little village church building was filled to capacity. When the meeting began an hour later, some eight hundred people were gathered to hear the man who had his education in Europe and Asia. Food vendors came from all over the area to take advantage of the large crowd. As the village chief looked out over the excited group, a wave of conviction swept over him.

"I cannot believe this is Yanga One on a Sunday morning," he thought to himself. "Since I have been saved, there has not been so much ungodly talk as there is this morning. What has happened to me?"

Instead of having the regular Sunday morning service, the time was given to Martin to speak. As he stepped to the platform, the crowd became silent.

"Fellow Banda tribesmen," the French-African speaker began, "I have been invited here today by my good friend, Chief Paul. Many of us knew him as Chief Ngonjo, but since he has received religion he has changed his name."

A number of people laughed at Martin's remarks. Chief Paul felt as though the speaker was making fun of his conversion. The conviction which he had felt earlier seemed to grow even greater as he thought of the wonderful life he had enjoyed since accepting Christ as his Savior.

Martin continued to speak. "I have been told that all of you are for the union, which, of course, gives you a contact with the outside world. This contact is good because it is through me, one of your own children. The foreign American missionary influence is slowly being wiped out. This kind of approach by an outside force is illegal as it takes away your religious freedom. It is all right if a person wants to believe in Christ. But I tell you, it is wrong when these same people say all others are lost forever if they do not accept Him. That is forced religion."

The more Martin spoke, the worse Chief Paul felt. He knew he was hearing things he did not believe, and all of this was replacing the village's Sunday morning worship service.

"Now, the union is your friend," Martin continued. "The people I represent recognize your poverty, and they want to do something about it. That is why I am here, to guide you in this good program."

One of the chiefs raised his hand to ask a question. Martin nodded to him to speak.

"When do we begin to get our trucks and buses? When will our sick people see the doctors you told us about? Many of us have already paid our money into the union, and we would like to know when we will see these things."

A clicking of tongues throughout the group indicated that many others had the same questions in mind. Martin Blanc responded to the chief's questions.

"As I have said many times, big changes like that do not come about in one day. It takes time to get the word back to the union leaders, and for them to send the equipment and personnel. It could even take a year before we begin to see results from your investments."

"A year?" someone shouted angrily. "You didn't tell us that when we gave you our money."

This was the first time Martin had talked about the time involved, and he was somewhat taken back by the negative attitude of his listeners. The people began to talk aloud with each other. Martin spoke out again.

"I will tell you what I can do for you. I will fly back to France just as soon as I can buy a place on the plane. The planes are usually filled this time of year, but I promise you I will leave as soon as possible and see what I can work out."

One of the men nearby stood up and raised his arm for silence.

"Quiet, everyone! Quiet! I want to ask Mr. Blanc something which has been in my heart since we started this meeting."

The man then turned to the union representative who, at that point, wished the meeting was over.

"Mr. Blanc, where have you put the money we have already paid to you for union dues? Have you sent it to France, or do you have it here in this country?"

"Let me explain this way," he began. "Some of your funds are still here with me and some I have sent to the union's headquarters. When I go see about the truck, buses and other equipment for your villages, I will take the money which I now have with me. The union must see that you are interested in following through with your financial commitments before they will send you the things which I have mentioned."

Desirous to get out of the village, Martin again spoke to the group.

"To show you how serious I am to speed up the progress of the development program offered to you by the union, I want to tell you of the decision which I have just made this very moment while standing here before you."

Silence gripped the large crowd as they waited to hear what the speaker had to say. Many were at the point of causing a disturbance, and Martin sensed this. He raised his head slightly, adjusted his glasses and began to speak.

"I know I promised my friend, Chief Paul, that I would come and spend the entire day speaking to you as a group and talking to you individually to answer your questions. Now, after seeing your concern this morning, I feel it is very important that you have representation as soon as possible in the union headquarters in France. I'm asking you to allow me to leave this meeting immediately so I can return to the post and pack my bags. I want to go to the capital city and catch the first plane possible. How does that sound to you? You will get action from the union when I plead your case with them. I will then return and personally direct the assignment of doctors as well as the shipment of the equipment."

"He is not telling the truth!" someone shouted from the back of the crowd. "Let me through. I have something to say to all of you."

Breaking through the people and walking down the center aisle came Bio, hobbling along with the help of her walking stick. Slung over her shoulder was a woven grass bag showing the top of a glass jar. She made her way to the platform and stood beside Martin. Her appearance was such a surprise that he was at a loss for words. He stood with his mouth open, looking at her.

"Kete Koli-Oko, you lie to these people," Bio said.

Chief Paul, sitting nearby, thought his mother had lost her mind. He got up to talk with her.

"Mama," he said quietly, "this man's name is Martin, not Kete Koli-Oko. Who is Kete Koli-Oko?"

"I am not as crazy as you may think, Paul. I was there when this man was born, and I heard his mother name him Kete Koli-Oko, which means 'my one little son.' He took the name of Martin Blanc when his father sent him to school in France. He never came back to his tribe until now. Only once did I contact him, and that was by a letter I sent to him. A schoolteacher wrote it for me. I had him promise he would never tell what was in the letter. That teacher died three years ago, so there are only two people alive who know what was written—Martin Blanc and I. I want to tell you the secret which has been kept these many years."

A deep hush captured the crowd. No one moved. Every ear strained to hear the old woman's words.

"When Martin's mother died over twenty years ago, she spoke her last words to me. She said, 'Bio, I give Kete Koli-Oko to you. He is to be responsible to you as his mother.'"

A flood of gasps and whispering went through the crowd. Martin stood with his head bowed, listening to what was being said.

"You mean he is my brother?" Chief Paul asked, surprised at the news.

"He is your brother, Paul. His mother gave him to me, but I never thought I would see him again."

The old lady reached into her woven bag and pulled out the jar. She opened it with her shaky hands and slowly pulled the paper from the inside. She held it high for all to see.

"I have a letter here which I received about four years ago. That same schoolteacher I told you about read it to me with the promise that he would keep its contents a secret. I want someone to read this letter to you now. It is from Martin Blanc!"

17

The
Reunion

As the union meeting was taking place at Yanga One, exciting things were also happening at Yanga Two. Pastor Kondo had just finished his sermon when one of the deacons stood to his feet.

"Pastor," he called out, surprising everyone at the sudden outburst, "I have something on my heart that I want to tell the church family. I have already settled it with the Lord, but I feel that I must tell the church as well."

Kondo recognized the deacon's request and gave him permission to speak. The middle-aged deacon stepped into the side aisle and made his way to the platform. The pastor stepped from the pulpit to allow the deacon to use it. He cleared his throat and began to speak.

"I do not know about all of you out there, but God has convicted me of what I have been saying about our missionaries these past two months. I am certain this morning as I stand before you that we Christians have been led into a satanic trap. We are guilty of taking our eyes off our God and following a man—Martin Blanc. I am confessing my wrongdoing to you as a church and ask you to forgive me."

The deacon then made his way over to Ken and Marge and put his arms around them. Ken felt Ouia's warm tears on his neck as he asked them to forgive him for what he had done.

"Of course you are forgiven, Ouia," Ken said, finding it impossible to hold back the tears. "Marge and I love you people, and we hold nothing against any of you."

As the deacon made his way back to his seat, others rose to their feet, asking permission to speak. Time slipped by without notice. One after another confessed publicly their part in the union's program, and their verbal attack on the missionaries. Marge squeezed Ken's hand tightly.

"I've never seen anything like this, Ken," she whispered to her husband. "God has won a great victory today at Yanga Two."

"He sure has, Honey," Ken replied. "I've been sitting here burdened for Chief Paul and the people of Yanga One. Oh, how I pray that they, too, will have their eyes opened to this satanic attack on them."

"If Bio has anything to do with it, you can be sure that Martin Blanc is having a hard time today at Yanga One. I can't help but believe that God is going to use that old woman to expose that evil program. Mr. Blanc is very clever, but he can't match the Lord's power when He begins to work."

"We have proof of that right here before us, Marge," said Ken, bringing their attention back to the meeting. "Our people look happy again. Praise the Lord for what He has done here today!"

The meeting ended and the entire congregation gathered around the two missionaries. Hand after hand poked through the crowd to shake their hands. So many people were talking at the same time that it was hard for them to understand any one person's conversation. But they didn't have to hear all that was being said. They already knew the hearts of their people. Ken and Marge finally got home shortly after three o'clock, tired but happy. God's blessings were more than either of them ever suspected in such a short time. It seemed that Ouia's words opened the windows of Heaven upon them as a church family.

Later that afternoon, as Ken and Marge were kneeling beside their bed, thanking the Lord for the great victory earlier in the day, a bicyclist arrived. The loud ring on the bicycle bell caught the missionaries' attention. Ken quickly went to the door.

"Hello, there. May I help you?"

"I have a message from Chief Paul. He wants you to come immediately. His mother is sick."

Without asking any further questions, Ken grabbed his medicine bag and headed for the truck, followed by Marge. The messenger put his bicycle in the back of the pickup and held it tightly as the truck headed down the driveway.

"I wonder what happened?" Marge asked as the truck turned onto the main road.

"I don't know, Honey," responded her husband. "Bio is an old woman and has been under a lot of stress lately."

"Like that walk through the jungle the other day," added Marge.

"Like that walk through the jungle," echoed Ken. "She's not up to doing things like that, but she felt she had to do it for the work's sake."

Thirty minutes later the truck entered the village of Yanga One. The missionary couple was surprised to see so many people milling about. The cloud of dust from the truck had been spotted several minutes before the couple actually arrived, and Chief Paul was waiting for them.

"Father," Ken prayed aloud as the truck came to a halt, "direct us in our visit."

Ken couldn't help but remember his last encounter with Chief Paul when he was told not only to leave the village, but also to return to America. He stepped from the truck, not knowing what to expect from the village chief and his people. Chief Paul stepped up and offered his hand to the missionary. Ken noted a sad look on the chief's face.

"It's too late, Dr. Simms," said the chief. "My mother just died. She is with Jesus."

"What happened to her, Chief Paul? Was she sick?" questioned Ken, walking with the chief to his hut.

"No, she was not sick. She had just finished giving her testimony of how God had saved her and changed her life when she sat down and closed her eyes. That was all there was to it."

"It was no doubt a heart attack, Chief," said the doctor, checking Bio's body to confirm her death. "She probably had no pain. Some people die easily like that."

"It was just as if she had finished a job she wanted to do. There was such a peaceful look on her face when we lifted her body from the chair to take it to my hut."

"Maybe she did finish a job, Chief Paul," said Ken, glancing at Marge standing nearby. "I don't know what happened this morning, but I have a feeling that things ended up the way your mother wanted them."

"You're right, Dr. Simms, and I want to ask your forgiveness for the way I have treated you both. You may be sure that everyone around this region is going to hear that I was wrong when I turned against you missionaries. Please sit down."

Ken and Marge sat down facing the village chief. Marge thought of the strange setting for a conversation—just the three of them in the chief's hut with Bio's body. Knowing that the missionaries would want to get home before it was too late, the chief began to share with them the thoughts of his heart.

"There is so much to tell you that I hardly know where to start," he said, rubbing his eyes. "As you know, I have been promoting the union's program which Martin Blanc brought to us. Earlier this week, I told my mother I was going to invite Martin to come and speak to the people here at Yanga One today. She opposed the idea, saying it was Sunday and the house of the Lord should not be used for that purpose. I went ahead and asked Martin to come and also invited the neighboring chiefs and their people."

Chief Paul stopped to wipe his eyes. "We started the meeting at nine o'clock this morning with about eight hundred people present. I could see immediately that Martin was in trouble. He made several statements that were not accepted, and soon an angry spirit could be seen among the crowd. When the pressure got too great for him, he asked to be excused. He said he wanted to return to the post, pack his bags and go immediately to the capital to take the first plane for France. He said he could get faster results for our people that way. Why, he even said that he himself would return with the doctors and the equipment and personally assign the doctors to their locations."

The chief stopped to swallow. Ken knew the village leader's grief made it difficult for him to speak.

"It was then that my dear mother made her way through the crowd. She came to the platform and told how she was with Martin's mother when she died. The two made a secret pact that my mother was to be Martin's mother. She then produced a letter which Martin had written to her about four years ago, telling how he was working with the Communists. He informed her how, after his schooling in France, he was sent to Moscow and was trained there in the ways of communism. This was arranged through the leaders of a Communist union in France. He made the mistake of telling her that there was no God, and that he would return to his people sometime in the future and teach them about communism."

"I see," said Ken, slowly nodding his head up and down. "When he got here, he found some opposition he didn't know was here."

"You are correct, Dr. Simms," replied the chief. "You missionaries were here, and he knew he had to get rid of you. But he did not know that my mother had believed in Jesus and that she was waiting for the right time to expose his evil plans before our people. Well, my mother had one of the young men read the letter. Martin would never have said the things he did if he had known that one day the letter would be read in his presence. He belittled the intelligence of his own people by saying that it is poor, unlearned people like them who provide good ground for communism. There were other things as well in the letter, but that was enough for the people to hear. My mother then told Martin to sit down while she shared some good news with the crowd. She then told how she chased me away from her hut in the jungle when I told her I had accepted Jesus as my Savior. She told in detail how she came unnoticed into the meeting in the chapel building and how she accepted Jesus privately in her heart. Of course, she had to tell of Kota and his attack on the mission station and how Tene got saved and went to Bible school."

Chief Paul stopped to laugh. "You would have been amused to hear of her trip to the Bible school and the meal she had with the missionaries. These past months have been happy ones for my mother. Jesus made the difference. She told how her life had been changed, and then she invited the unsaved in the crowd to accept Jesus as their Savior. I do not believe there was a dry eye when she finished and sat down."

The three sat in silence for a moment before the chief spoke again. "Oh, I meant to tell you, Dr. Simms. Martin Blanc is over in my mother's hut. He wants to talk with you."

18

Confrontation
at Yanga
One

Ken and Marge Simms entered the small hut located near the center of the village. Martin Blanc rose to greet them. He seemed pleasant enough, but then, he was trained to gain the friendship of people by being kind and courteous to them.

Marge thought of his lack of kindness to them when he first arrived. At that time there was no need to be nice to them. In fact, he wanted to do all he could to discourage them and cause them to leave.

"Hello, Dr. Simms," spoke the young man, reaching out to shake hands.

"Hello, Mr. Blanc," replied Ken. "How are you?"

After exchanging greetings, the three sat down at Martin's suggestion.

"Thank you for coming, Dr. Simms. I told Chief Paul that I wanted to talk with you when you arrived, and he told me to use his mother's house as a meeting place. I am sure the chief thinks I am going to confess to you my wrongdoings and ask forgiveness, but I am not. Neither do I have any intention of doing so later."

Marge could see more and more the ruthless attitude of the man sitting before them.

"This whole thing reminds me of two buffalo bulls fighting each other. We want the same territory. For the time being, you have driven me out and have gained control. I will go away, but you may be sure that I will be back. You see, I want this territory. I will not give it up that easily."

"But I am not fighting you, Mr. Blanc. I haven't even talked against you before our people. I had suspicions about you and what you represent, but I always like to make sure I know what I'm doing before I do it."

"If it wasn't you, then who was it? Somebody has been undermining me this past week."

"It's the Lord. He's the One Who has been opposing you. You've been deceiving His people, and the Spirit of God has convicted them of their participation in your program. No, Mr. Blanc," emphasized the doctor, "you're really battling the Lord, not us. The battle is His."

The light-skinned man stared at Ken as though he was planning his next verbal attack. The silence in the hut caused a chill to run through Marge's body. When he spoke again, Martin did so in a quiet, deliberate manner.

"I will tell you what I can do for you if you will cooperate even a little bit with me."

Ken wanted to speak, but he remained silent to listen to Martin, who was leaning forward in his chair.

"All you have to do, Dr. Simms, is be friendly with me. Invite me out to the mission station now and then, maybe to have a meal with you. When you have opportunity to do so, promote my union program before the people. Make them believe that it will take time to do what I have promised them—maybe even two years. That is all I am asking you to do."

"But—" Ken began to speak, but Martin continued.

"Now, if you will do that for me, then I can promise you that, in a very short time, I will see to it that the mission church and the chapel building here at Yanga One are filled with people. I will make church attendance mandatory for all union members. How does that sound, Dr. Simms?"

Ken looked at the man sitting across from him. The verse in 1 John 2:15 flashed through his mind: "Love not the world, neither the things that are in the world. If any man love the world, the love of the Father is not in him." He looked hard into Martin's eyes.

"That's compromise, Mr. Blanc. I could never overlook sin just to see you fill the Lord's house with unregenerate people. You are robbing your own people. You talk about helping them in their poverty and, at the same time, have devised a program to provide you with monetary gain from what little they earn. Then, too, you are attempting to establish a foothold for your 'Red' leaders in France who, in turn, are under the Communist regime in Russia."

As Ken stood up to leave, he turned to speak to Martin.

"Before Marge and I leave, Mr. Blanc, I want to tell you that Jesus died on the cross for your sins. He will forgive you and save you if you will accept Him as your Savior. Would you like to receive Him, Mr. Blanc?"

"Get out!" screamed the angry French-African, jumping to his feet. "Get out of here and leave me alone!"

Marge walked close to her husband as they left the hut. "Whew! I'm sure glad to get out of there," she whispered, holding tightly to Ken's arm.

"Well, you have finally come out," called Chief Paul from the small grass-roofed chapel. "Where's Martin? Is he coming?"

Ken waited until he got closer to the chief before he spoke.

"I don't think he'll be joining us, Chief. He's very angry with me. In fact, he told Marge and me to leave the hut."

The missionaries and the chief walked slowly to the blue pickup. Ken sensed that his friend had something upon his heart.

"Chief Paul," Ken began, "is there something we can do for you or your people? We loved your mother dearly, and we want you to feel free to ask us if you know of ways we can be of help to you."

"Well, there is something you can do for me, Dr. Simms," said Chief Paul hesitantly. "I really would not ask you to do this; but since you want me to, I will."

"What is it, Chief?" asked Ken.

"Would you be so kind as to bring Tene from Bible school for the funeral? I know it will take you all night to go and come back, but you could make it for the funeral service. We will wait for your return."

Ken looked at Marge, who smiled and nodded her head slowly, and then replied, "We'll be happy to go for you, Chief Paul."

"I will send four of my strongest men with you, Dr. Simms. If you have any trouble on the road, they will help you."

Just then the chief spotted Martin Blanc walking with two other men toward the road.

"Martin!" he called, cupping his hands to his mouth. "If you are going back to the post, here is a ride for you. You can ride in Dr. Simms's truck."

The Communist agent tried to smile as he waved back to the village leader. "Thank the doctor for me, Chief. I want to stop in some of the villages along the way."

"I knew he would not ride with you, Dr. Simms. I just wanted to hear what he had to say," the chief said to the startled couple.

As they drove away from Yanga One with their four companions in the back of the truck, Ken noticed several men making their way to the edge of the village where they would soon begin digging a new grave beside that of Kota's—the grave of the chief's mother.

Ken and Marge stopped at Yanga One to inform Pastor Kondo of Bio's death. The pastor set out for Yanga One almost immediately. One of the station workmen filled the gas tank on the pickup. He also filled the four, twenty-liter gas cans and securely fastened them in the back of the truck. Marge put some clothing in a suitcase while Ken busied himself getting his tool box and an extra spare wheel into the truck. As always, an axe and shovel were put in, along with a coil of rope. Within twenty minutes, the pickup pulled out of the mission station driveway and headed for its destination 180 miles away.

"It's going to be chilly traveling at night," Ken said, looking over at Marge in the fading light. "I'm glad you thought to bring that pillow and blanket so you can at least get some sleep."

"I brought several blankets for the men too," responded Marge. "It'll be plenty cold for them tonight too. Maybe we can stop halfway and make some coffee. I had one of the men put that camping pressure stove in the truck."

"How fortunate I am," thought Ken, "to have such a thoughtful wife." A slight smile appeared on his face as he thought of Marge.

Mile after mile, the couple rode along in silence, thinking of the tremendous turn of events that day at Yanga One and Two. Finally Marge spoke as she watched the road ahead pass beneath them.

"These have been exciting days, Ken," she said above the roar of the motor. "I know a lot of things have happened at Yanga One, but I don't think Yanga Two is far behind when it comes to things happening."

"That's right, Honey," agreed Ken as he kept his eyes glued to the road. "And to think that God has privileged us to be a part of it."

As they came around a bend in the road, Marge saw it immediately. The huge, spotted cat turned and looked into the headlights of the approaching pickup. Its eyes reflected the truck's lights like two giant, flashing emeralds.

"It's a leopard!" shouted Marge. "You're going to hit it!"

Ken braked the pickup, realizing that in the back he had four men who were unprotected from the dangerous beast. The large, spotted cat stood its ground. Slowly it made its way toward the truck.

"Father, protect the men," Marge prayed aloud as the leopard approached.

"The horn!" Ken thought to himself. In a flash his hand landed squarely on the horn button. The blast sent the giant cat reeling backwards. At the same time, Ken put the truck into gear and moved forward, blowing the horn as he went. The leopard turned and, with a great leap, was off the road and into the tall grass. Ken stepped on the accelerator and left dirt flying as he sped off into the night.

"Thank You, Father," prayed Ken.

"Yes, thank You, Lord," responded Marge as she glanced through the back window to see how their four traveling companions were doing. To her surprise, there were four smiling faces staring into the cab. Each of the men was talking to the missionaries, unaware that their voices couldn't be heard through the glass. Ken stuck his head out of the window and called to them.

"What are you saying? We can't hear you."

One of the men poked his head over the side of the cab. "We said, 'Thank you for running faster than that leopard.' But we want to know—what made that animal make such a terrible noise? We've never heard one growl like that before."

"Tell them, Honey," said Marge, laughing quietly. "Let's hear you explain how you made that leopard growl by pushing the button on the steering wheel."

"Uh—uh—wait until we stop for coffee down the road. I'll tell you then," answered Ken, turning to make a face at his wife.

Three miles down the road was a wide place where they would stop. It would be a spot about which they would talk for years to come. It was there in the middle of the night where a man named Death found life.

19

Death Becomes Life

The bright light from the full moon high in the sky cast a strange array of shadows about the village of Yanga One. Two men sat together just outside the little grass-roofed chapel where the body of Bio, the chief's mother, lay in a hastily built casket. The men had their heads bowed, praying.

"Father, please save Koui. Give Dr. and Mrs. Simms the opportunity to witness to him. He is the only one still unsaved in his family. Lord, we are asking You to work in Koui's heart and cause him to turn to You."

Chief Paul lifted his head and looked out across his village. The death of his mother had brought many visitors into Yanga One. Small fires dotted the village, with each fire surrounded by blanket-covered forms trying to keep warm in the cold night air. The village leader turned to the man sitting beside him.

"I am so glad you came to be with me, Pastor Kondo." A smile spread across the chief's face as he spoke. "I find it difficult to believe all that has happened since the day I chased you and Mr. Davis out of my village. It all seems like a dream, but a very wonderful dream."

Chief Paul stopped and stared at the bright silver moon hanging in the dark sky.

"There was a time, Pastor Kondo, when both you and I would be afraid of nights like this. We would be out dancing all night, hoping our screaming and the noise of the drums would scare away the evil spirits."

"How true, Chief Paul, but God has miraculously set us free from all that. Praise His name, we are now new creatures in Christ."

"To think," said the chief, looking toward the casket, "that my mother is now in the presence of the Lord. What a great change took place in her life after her conversion. I will never forget her testimony yesterday afternoon right before she died."

Kondo stood up to stretch his legs. "I know of at least nineteen people who accepted Christ as a result of what she said."

"Thank the Lord," whispered the chief. "I spoke to several also who believed in Jesus."

Pastor Kondo sat down again and placed his hand on the chief's shoulder.

"Chief Paul," he said, looking past his friend out into the village, "let's pray some more for Koui. I have an unusual burden on my heart for that man since you told me about him tonight. I am glad he was one of those chosen to travel with the Simmses. Dr. Simms will use every opportunity he can to witness to the men."

The two leaders once again bowed their heads, and Kondo began to pray. At that very moment, many miles away, Koui was sitting beside a small fire some distance behind Ken Simms's pickup, listening to the doctor tell the well-known story once again.

"Is that really all there is to it, Dr. Simms?" asked the inquisitive African.

"Yes, that's all there is to it, Koui," responded Ken. The flickering flames showed the serious look on the American's face.

"My wife has tried to talk with me," said Koui, "but I have always shut her up by threatening to beat her. Even my three children tried to tell me about Jesus, but I did the same with them. I must admit, though, since they accepted Christ, all of them have been living differently than before. I do not even feel like part of them anymore."

Koui hung his head as his own words lay heavily upon his heart. The other three men sat in silence, listening. They had told Ken in an earlier conversation that they were saved and actively serving the Lord. Marge's heart ached for Koui, who was fighting a battle that very moment.

Finally Koui looked up at Ken, shaking his head to indicate he couldn't make that all-important decision.

"I can't do it, Dr. Simms. What will my gods do to me? I am afraid to reject them. They will kill me if I do."

"No, they won't kill you, Koui. They'll have no power over you. Receive Jesus as your Savior. Confess your sins to God and ask Him to forgive you. Please, Koui, won't you do it now?"

The tall African stood up and turned to face the darkened jungle, which seemed to hover over them. His booming voice rang out, echoing back from the forest.

"I cannot stand being afraid of you all the time!" he shouted. "I am tired of living in fear and anger. I am through with you, Satan."

A chill ran up Marge's back. Never before had she heard anything like this in her Christian life. Ken and the three African Christians sat and watched. The doctor was aware that the three men knew the battle that was going on within the heart of their friend. As Koui turned to the fire, his face was wet with tears. Quickly he dropped to his knees, and, between sobs, asked Ken to help him pray.

"God," he prayed, "my heart is filled with wickedness. I want it to be a clean heart. Take away the fears which have bothered me for many years. I want You to be my God—just like You are to these friends here with me. I believe that Jesus died for me. I want Him to be my Savior. God, make me Your child.

For several moments there was a complete silence as Koui knelt with his head bowed. Ken knew that his new brother in Christ was silently praying in his heart. Finally, Koui looked up. His face beamed with happiness.

"What can I say?" he asked, crying and laughing at the same time. "I feel different. The weight is gone from my heart. I feel like new, Dr. Simms."

He reached his hand out to his three friends. If he shook their hands once, he shook them six times. All four were talking at the same time. Finally Koui turned to shake the hands of Ken and Marge.

"Before we continue any farther tonight, Dr. Simms, there is something I must tell you," Koui said.

Not knowing what to expect, Ken held up his hand for all to listen. Again there was silence, broken only by the sounds of the surrounding jungle.

"My friends," said Koui in a clear, stern voice, "our village has not been the same since our chief accepted Jesus as his Savior. Many of our people, as well as those from other villages, have lived different lives since becoming Christians. Tonight that has been my experience. I know now what Kadja and the children have been telling me. I am not only a new man, but I am a new man with a new name."

He stopped for a few seconds, then continued.

"Koui means death. I am not dead anymore. I am alive. From now on I am Fini. That means life, Dr. Simms. I want everyone to know that I have new life in Jesus."

They all shook hands with Fini and then got into the truck to continue their journey to meet Tene at Bible school. Even the pickup seemed to take on new life as it purred along the sandy clay road. Marge talked like a chirping bird about what had taken place behind them on the road. Ken looked at his watch.

"If we don't have any trouble, we can be back by eight o'clock in the morning. I don't think I could be sleepy even if I tried!"

Meanwhile, back at Yanga One, Chief Paul and Kondo had just finished praying for Koui and had seated themselves beside one of the fires to make some coffee. Several of those who had been sleeping under blankets sat up to drink with the two men. A visiting village chief came over to join them. So as not to awaken the others sleeping nearby, they spoke to one another in a whisper.

A loud cry startled the entire village. Kondo jumped to his feet at the first word of alarm.

"Fire! The chapel is on fire!"

What seemed to be a small, red glow grew to a leaping, flaming torch in just a matter of seconds.

"Water! Someone bring water!" one of the men called, running toward a hut.

"My mother's body!" shouted Chief Paul, racing toward the flaming building.

Kondo, who was much younger and faster, ran past the chief and, without any hesitation, burst into the flaming building. He picked up the white wooden box and turned to go out the way he had entered. But the spreading flames blocked the doorway. He moved quickly to the far end of the building where there were fewer flames. There, eight feet above the floor, was a ventilation window. Kondo jumped and pulled himself to the ledge, calling to several men standing some twenty feet away.

"Come quickly! One of you get up here. I'm going back down to push the casket up to you."

Kondo dropped back into the burning building, and with brute strength, lifted the box high enough to enable the man above to pull it through the opening. Quickly it was handed down to the men outside who carried it a safe distance. The man in the window jumped to the ground to make room for Kondo on the ledge.

Chief Paul stood in the crowd which had gathered to see the

heroic efforts of the men. All eyes were fastened on the window at the end of the building. The flames seemed to be everywhere on the roof.

"There he is!" someone shouted as Kondo's head and arms appeared above the ledge. The room behind him was a roaring, red inferno.

"He's on fire! His clothes are burning!"

Flames could be seen leaping around Kondo as he fought to get his body up on the ledge. With what seemed to be a last surge of strength, Kondo pushed himself to the ledge and fell to the ground below. As the Africans quickly smothered his burning clothes in blankets, Kondo's body went limp.

"Father," sobbed Chief Paul, standing beside the white wooden casket, "I must confess that I cannot understand all that is happening to us. All I know is that You are perfect in all You do. Help me to trust You, Lord, and please, don't let Kondo die."

At that very moment, Ken Simms was informing Tene about Bio's death and the fact that Chief Paul wanted him to come home for the funeral. Little could they know the tragic news that awaited them at Yanga One.

20

A
Strange
Request

The night air made the men shiver. Ken got more blankets from Bill Dykes for the men, but the chilly wind from the moving truck seemed to cut right through the blankets. They traveled without any difficulty and were on schedule to arrive at Yanga One by eight o'clock.

The warm morning sun was a welcome sight to the shivering men. Tene, who had been nursing a cold, sat in the cab with Ken and Marge. His eyes were red from crying and a lack of sleep.

"Not much farther now," said Ken as they approached the mission station. "I think I'll stop and get Tessi. We'll surprise Pastor Kondo by taking her with us to Yanga One."

The pastor's wife put a few things in a small plywood suitcase and got into the cab with Ken and Marge. Since the sun was now shining brightly, Tene got into the back of the truck with the other men. The pickup again moved rapidly toward its destination.

"There's Yanga One!" called Fini. "But something is wrong. The chapel roof is gone. There's been a fire."

Within a moment, the pickup pulled into the village. There, in front of Chief Paul's house, rested the white wooden casket. A large crowd was gathered around the chief's dwelling. Someone called Chief Paul and told him Dr. Simms had arrived. He appeared from the low, narrow door just as Ken stopped the truck. The tall village leader walked quickly toward the pickup. Tears filled his eyes as he approached the missionary doctor.

"Dr. Simms," he said in a broken voice, "something terrible has happened to Pastor Kondo. He is badly burned and needs your help. Come quickly. He is in my house."

Without any further exchange of words, Ken followed the chief into the familiar hut. Hanging on a wire in the center of the room was a kerosene pressure lamp which cast eerie shadows about the dried, mud-block building. Lying near the wall on the far side of the round room was Kondo. Ken knelt beside him. Marge stood behind her husband.

"Marge, my flashlight is in the glove compartment. Could you get it for me, please?"

Ken turned to the village leader. "Chief Paul, would you please go with Mrs. Simms and bring my medicine bag?"

Ken looked closely at the African pastor. He lay motionless and near death. On his face was frozen the expression of pain he experienced before he lapsed into a coma.

Ken prayed as he worked on his African brother. After doing what he could for the time being, the doctor stepped out of the hut for a breath of fresh air. Marge followed close behind.

"How bad is he, Ken?" she asked in a whisper.

"He's badly burned over half his body. I've given him some antibiotics to help fight off infection. If he can hold his own for a couple of days, I'll transport him to the general hospital in the capital."

"Do you have the things to treat him now?" questioned the young wife.

"Not here," answered Ken, "but I do at the station. I'll wait here a couple of hours and then go home for the supplies I need. You can watch him while I'm gone."

Chief Paul came out of his house and joined the couple.

"Do you have any idea how the fire started, Chief Paul?" Ken asked, looking in the direction of the destroyed chapel building.

"Yes, I do," answered the leader. "One of my men told me that he saw one of Martin's followers near the chapel just before the fire."

"You don't think he . . . ?" Marge's voice trailed off to a whisper.

"My heart tells me that Martin is responsible for the fire. I do not think he knew that my mother's casket was inside. I am sure, though, that he did not want to harm anyone."

"But why would he do it?" asked Marge, with a puzzled look.

"Martin knew what that chapel means to our people. He knows, too, that the Lord and His people are his biggest opposition. I am sure he destroyed the building to try to discourage us."

"We're just going to have to pray for him even more than we have been, Chief Paul," said Ken, turning to go back to the hut to take another look at Kondo.

A short time later, as Ken came back out of the hut, Chief Paul approached him.

"Dr. Simms, your wife tells me you will be going back to Yanga Two in a short time for more medical supplies."

"That's correct, Chief," responded Ken. "There are some things at home I need for my treatment of Kondo."

"What I want to ask, Dr. Simms, is whether or not you will give a message to the people who came here for my mother's burial? We really should have the funeral this morning."

"Of course, I'll do that, Chief Paul. Why don't we go ahead with the service now?"

The respected leader summoned two of his men and told them to call the people together at the edge of the village where the open grave was waiting to receive the casket containing Bio's body. Within minutes, several hundred men, women and children were making their way to the graveside.

Tene got some of the young men to help him carry the white wooden box. As he walked along, he thought again of the tremendous change that had taken place in his own life and how Bio was responsible for a good share of it.

"I have asked Tene to lead us in the singing of some hymns," Chief Paul told the crowd. "He has been away to Bible school and his teachers have shown him how to lead singing the right way. Everyone watch him closely."

Tene felt mixed emotions as he stepped up on the mound of dirt beside the grave. He was sorrowing because of Bio's death and Pastor Kondo's accident, but yet rejoicing that Bio was now with the Lord and that he, too, knew and loved the Lord and was preparing for His work. In a strong, clear voice, Tene announced the first hymn.

"Let's sing 'Blessed Assurance, Jesus Is Mine!' "

As the Bible school student beat out the time with his right arm, Ken found it difficult to sing. He, too, had mixed emotions. The stress of dealing with Martin Blanc, Bio's death, Fini's conversion and now the near fatal accident of his close friend, Kondo, was almost too much for any human to take in such a short space of time. He glanced over at Fini standing with his wife and children, and he was strengthened with a new surge of encouragement.

"Thank You, Lord," he whispered. "They are now a complete family in You."

Tene led in two more hymns and then turned the service over to his father, Chief Paul. The chief stood with his hands on the casket.

"My friends, many of you heard my mother's testimony yesterday before she died. Dr. Simms will be talking to us in just a short while about the Word of God, but I wanted to say something to you who have come for my mother's funeral."

The large crowd listened to every word spoken by the chief. Several could be heard clicking their tongues, indicating their agreement with what Chief Paul was saying. While the funeral service was going on, Marge quietly sat beside Kondo, who was beginning to show signs of regaining consciousness.

"Lord," she prayed softly, "please spare Kondo's life. Don't let him be crippled from this accident."

The pastor's wife, Tessi, sat on the edge of the grass mat on which her husband lay. She, too, was in constant prayer for her loved one.

Meanwhile, outside under the flamboyant tree, the village chief continued to speak to the colorfully clad audience.

"The woman whom many of you knew from the jungle hut out there is not the same woman that we here at Yanga One knew the past several months. My mother, Bio, became a new woman because of what Jesus did for her. The message you are going to hear today from Dr. Simms is the message that my mother would have asked to have preached at her funeral. The words you hear will represent the plea which would have come from her heart. I ask you to listen carefully to each word that the man of God has for us today."

Ken climbed to the top of the mound of dirt. The open grave was just to the right of him. He opened the Bible and began to read from the fourteenth chapter of John. He spoke about the peace of God that can come to a troubled heart by accepting Christ. He talked of the home in Heaven that Christ is preparing for His own. Finally he focused on verse 6. His voice seemed to penetrate every heart as he read loudly and clearly, "Jesus saith unto him, I am the way, the truth, and the life: no man cometh unto the Father, but by me."

As Ken gave the invitation, men and women stood up throughout the crowd and made their way to the graveside. Chief

Paul's eyes were filled with tears as the scene before him reminded him of another graveside invitation not many months before.

"Perhaps God will raise up another Tene," he whispered to himself.

Ken Simms finished the invitation and closed in prayer.

"Heavenly Father, please help those who believed in Jesus as their Savior today to live for You. Give them the strength to be a testimony for You among their own people. And, Lord," he continued, "lay Your healing hand upon Pastor Kondo's body. Raise him up, Father, that he may return to do Your work."

When Ken said amen, a murmur of amens could be heard throughout the crowd. Tene and several of the believers took aside the ones who made decisions, so they could counsel and pray with them. The crowd moved back into the village as several of the men lowered the casket into the grave and began to fill in the hole with dirt. Ken and Chief Paul walked together toward the chief's hut. As they approached the door, Marge appeared in the doorway.

"Kondo has regained consciousness," she said, beaming from ear to ear. "He asked me about the fire. When he learned one of Martin's men may have started it, he asked immediately for Martin to come and see him."

"I wonder why he wants to see Martin," spoke the chief, looking somewhat surprised. "If it is all right for him to have visitors, Dr. Simms, I will send a runner out for Martin right now."

"I'll have a look at him, Chief," responded Ken, "but I'm quite sure it will be all right."

As Ken and the chief entered the hut, both of them were thinking the same thought: What results could come from a meeting between Martin and Pastor Kondo—a man who had almost lost his life in a fire and the man who had ordered the fire to be set?

21
No
Hard
Feelings

The sound of handclapping told Martin Blanc that someone outside wanted to talk with him. The French-African pushed away from the table where he was busy writing a letter.

"I hear you!" he shouted to the waiting messenger. "I'm coming."

He opened the door and stepped out to face Chief Paul's runner.

"Hello. What can I do for you?"

"Chief Paul sent me, Mr. Blanc. He says he wants to see you immediately. He did not know where you were, so I have been asking for you in every village along the road. When I arrived here, they told me that you had asked to stay in the village guest house for a couple of days."

"What does Chief Paul want to see me about?" asked Martin.

"I don't know, Mr. Blanc, but he was very serious when he sent me to find you. He told me to go as far as was necessary to give you the message. I am glad I only had to travel this far. It is only an hour's ride by bicycle."

"Tell him I will be there by evening. I don't think I can get there any sooner."

With the message for his chief, the runner returned to Yanga One, arriving just a few minutes before Martin Blanc, who came by bicycle. Chief Paul met the summoned visitor as he made his way into the village.

"Greetings, Chief Paul. I received your mesage and came as soon as I could. I had to wait for one of the villagers to return with his bicycle. I thought that would be the easiest way to come."

As the two men conversed, Ken Simms arrived from Yanga Two with the medical supplies he needed, as well as three folding camp cots and mosquito nets. He knew that it would be several days before Kondo could be moved, and he and Marge didn't want to leave their patient for any length of time. The missionaries would stay in Bio's hut while the chief, Kondo and Tene would stay in the chief's hut.

Ken got out of the truck and shook Martin's hand.

"Hello, Mr. Blanc. How are you?"

"I am fine, Dr. Simms."

"Martin," called Chief Paul, "the reason I asked you to come is because of a request from Pastor Kondo."

The chief then quickly told the union official what had happened. Martin seemed to be shaken when he heard that the casket of the chief's mother was in the chapel and that Kondo's life was in the balance because he was trapped in the fire trying to save the body.

"And you say that Kondo wants to see me?" asked Martin.

"Yes, he requested to see you. Dr. Simms is checking him now to see if he can have a visitor," replied the chief.

Ken appeared from the chief's hut.

"He seems to be improving already. He's a very sick man, Mr. Blanc. Please don't upset him in any way. If you see he's getting tired, tell him that you will finish the conversation with him tomorrow. You may go in now."

Martin quietly entered the large, round room. The pastor never moved his head, but remained still, staring at the grass roof above.

"Hello," he said in a weak voice.

"Hello, Kondo," responded the seemingly subdued visitor. "How do you feel?"

"Not too well," answered Kondo. "Come closer so you can hear me."

Martin seemed almost afraid to get near the pastor. He felt an uneasiness run through him as he sat in a chair near the grass mat.

"They said you asked to see me."

"I do want to see you. I know I am very weak, so I will get to the heart of what I want to say."

Martin waited for Kondo's next words. He was not very anxious to hear any further discussion from the sick man, but he knew he had no choice but to listen.

100

"You are responsible for the fire that destroyed the chapel. Is that not true?"

A long silence followed Kondo's question. Martin Blanc hung his head and stared at the clay floor.

Kondo spoke again. "Martin, answer me."

In a shaking voice the visitor answered. Even in his condition, Kondo sensed the effort it took for Martin to answer.

"Yes, Kondo, I sent one of my men to start the fire."

"Why, Martin?"

"I did it to destroy the meeting place of the Christians. I thought it would discourage them and help my cause."

"Did you know that the body of Chief Paul's mother was in there, waiting for the funeral service the next morning?"

"No, I didn't know that then."

"Martin, there is something terribly wrong in your heart. You really need to confess your sins and accept Jesus as your Savior."

Martin seemed to ignore what the pastor had said.

"I was told you saved the body from the fire and got trapped in the building. They said that only a last, all-out effort on your part to push yourself out the window saved you from dying in the fire."

"I cannot remember what happened, Martin, but I am positive that God spared my life. Maybe He did it just so I could have this conversation with you."

Kondo stopped to catch his breath, then continued. "I don't know if I will live through this, Martin, but even if I don't, I want to tell you that I forgive you. I hold no hard feelings toward you. I mean that, Martin."

The pastor's visitor had not been prepared for this response from Kondo. A flood of tears came coursing down his cheeks. He slipped off the chair and onto his knees. He wished he could reach out and touch his friend, but knew he couldn't.

"Kondo," he cried, "please forgive me for what I have done. I didn't mean to hurt anyone like this. Will you forgive me, Kondo?"

"I have told you, Martin, that I have already forgiven you. But your sins still remain before God. Why not let Him forgive them too? He is willing to do it for you. Will you confess your sins to Him?"

"Yes, I will, Kondo. I want to be clean before God."

"Then believe now that Jesus died to forgive you and save you from your sins. He loves you, Martin. He wants to give you eternal life and make you His child. Will you let Him right now?"

"God," Martin cried, "forgive me of my terrible ways. I am such an evil man and I need your help. I believe that Jesus is your Son and that He died for me. God, save me from my sins."

A long silence followed, broken only by Martin's sobs and short prayers to his new Heavenly Father. Kondo quietly thanked the Lord in his heart for the salvation of Martin Blanc. After a short time, the new Christian spoke to his pastor friend.

"I am saved, Kondo. I am a new man. It is a wonderful feeling. I cannot explain it."

"I know what you are talking about, Martin. I have been a Christian for six years now. Thank the Lord for your salvation."

"I have to tell the others, Kondo. You are probably very tired and need some rest. Would you mind if I went out and told those who are here in the village that I am now a Christian?"

"Go ahead, Martin. They will be glad to hear it."

As he stood up, Martin looked down at his friend. "Thank you, Kondo. Thank you for your love for me. I am going to ask God to spare your life."

The new believer turned and made his way to the door. He could hardly wait to break the good news of what God had done for him. As he stepped outside, he noticed the concerned looks on the faces of the Simmses and Chief Paul. A wide grin spread across his face.

"Stop looking so worried, everybody," he called. "I am one of you now. I have just accepted Christ as my Savior. I am a Christian too."

Those who heard Martin began hugging each other in their excitement. Chief Paul was the first to respond.

"Thank the Lord, Martin. God has answered our prayers. You are one of us."

"Thank the Lord, Martin," echoed Ken, putting his arm around the shoulder of the man who, at one time, had tried to drive him from the country. "You are now my brother."

Others began to approach Martin to shake his hand and tell him how happy they were to hear of his salvation. Ken slipped into the hut to check on Kondo. He found his patient sleeping soundly, a peaceful look on his face. For some reason, Ken felt that his patient was going to make it.

Late that night, long after the villagers had retired, Ken lay wide awake, going over the blessings of the past several hours. Sleep seemed to be nowhere in sight.

"What was that?" he whispered to himself. Again he heard it. Someone was at the door.

"Who can it be at this time of night?" he thought to himself as he slipped out from under the mosquito net and put on his robe and shoes. He made his way quietly to the door and opened it. There before him in the moonlight stood Tene and Martin.

"Hello, my friends. What can I do for you?"

"We are sorry to bother you this late, Dr. Simms," said Tene, "but Martin and I have been talking and praying together since it got dark. We have come to ask you a question. It is so important to Martin that he did not want to wait until morning to ask you."

"That's all right, Tene. I wasn't sleeping anyway."

Ken turned to Martin who was eagerly waiting to ask his question.

"What is it, Martin, that you want to ask me?"

"Dr. Simms," said Martin nervously, "I don't know how to say what is on my heart."

The educated African hesitated, seeming to search for just the right words.

"Tene and I have been talking about it tonight, Dr. Simms. Is it possible for me to enroll in Bible school?"

Ken looked at the serious face before him. Bits of Martin's life flashed through the missionary's mind as he tried to form an answer to give the new Christian. Martin waited patiently for the reply.

22

To
the
Capital

"What did you say to him?" Marge asked her husband after he related to her the conversation that had just taken place outside the hut. The young wife had awakened when Ken opened the door to go out. She lay there, hearing only the muffled sounds of their voices.

"I told him to come see me when we both had time to talk the whole thing over. There are some things in his life which need to be clarified."

"Like what, Honey?" asked Marge, propping herself up on her cot.

"Well, he is reported to have three wives. Two are here and one is in France. Then, too, I'd like to hear about his involvement with the Communist party as well as his handling of the funds taken from the Banda tribe. Please don't think that I'm building a case against him. He's a brother in Christ, but I want to hear about these things before any commitment is made to him."

"You're right, Ken. I didn't think about all those things. I was so happy about his conversion that I momentarily overlooked his past connections."

"We both know there's forgiveness for what he has done," continued Ken, "but we are dealing with the Lord's work. There are Scriptural principles which God has given to us as guidelines for His work."

Morning came quickly for the tired couple. Ken had been up several times during the night to check on Pastor Kondo, who seemed to be increasing in strength.

Marge fixed their breakfast over a small pressure kerosene

stove. As they sat and ate their meal in the privacy of the small hut, Martin Blanc's name came up in their conversation.

"I really don't believe he is legally married to the two Banda women," said Ken. "If that is the case, then that relationship would be rather simple to sever. We'll just have to wait and see."

A clapping of hands told the missionaries that someone outside wanted to see them. Ken went to the door and saw Martin standing there.

"Good morning, Dr. Simms. I wanted to come and talk with you and Mrs. Simms alone this morning. May I come in?"

"Oh, please do, Martin. Would you like a cup of coffee?" asked Ken, opening a folding chair he had brought back with him from Yanga Two the day before.

"Yes, thank you. Maybe that will help me. I guess my stomach is a bit nervous over what is on my mind."

Marge sensed that the new Christian was troubled and needed to talk with someone who understood. Martin sat down beside the small table and began to unfold his thoughts as he fumbled nervously with the spoon in his hands.

"You people are about the only ones I know with whom I can talk about these things. I hope you don't mind taking the time to listen to me."

"Martin, that's one of the reasons we are here. We want to help you people with your problems and share your burdens," spoke Ken as he poured coffee into Martin's cup.

"First of all, I know I am a Christian," Martin said. "God has given me joy and peace like nothing I have known before. The thing that bothers me now is the entanglements in my life. I came last night asking if it were possible for me to go to Bible school. Tene tried to discourage me from asking such a question, but I was so excited about getting started in the Lord's work that it just seemed to pop out. Then, too, I wanted to share some of my problems with you and did not think I could wait until morning."

"I understand," said Ken, nodding his head slowly. "Then you probably have changed your mind about Bible school."

"Yes, I have. At least for now," replied Martin, sipping at his coffee. "The two Banda women that you met are not really married to me. In my heart, I have already settled that problem. When I get back to the post later this afternoon, I will send them back to their villages. My legal wife is in France. She is French and is not a Christian. I plan to return to France as soon as possible. I know she will not understand the change in me and it will be a very difficult marriage, but I know that is what God wants me to do. She is my responsibility, and I will do my best to live a testimony for Jesus before her."

"Do you know any Christians in France, Martin?" asked Marge.

"No, I don't. I thought perhaps you people would know someone there who could help me."

"Where is your wife living in France?" questioned Ken.

"She is right in Paris. We have an apartment there."

"That's wonderful," exclaimed Marge. "We have a number of missionaries living in and around Paris. They would be happy to help you in any way possible. Just think, you've already got friends there who will take in you and your wife like family."

"I feel better already," responded Martin. "I had no idea that you had missionaries that close to us."

"That's the Lord working things out for you," replied Ken. "Tell me, what about your relationship with the Communist party?"

"I was coming to that, Dr. Simms. I was appointed as one of the leaders of the Communist Workers' Union in France. Evidently they saw some leadership qualities in me, for they sent me to Moscow for training. It was there I was informed of their desire to make inroads into Africa. They had African students from all over the continent training there for this same purpose. There were different approaches, but the end results would all be the same— the advancement of communism and the breaking down of the morals of the countries, starting with the individual families."

"Then your assignment was to win the Banda tribe over to the doctrine of communism?" questioned Ken.

"Correct," answered Martin. "I was to indoctrinate as many of the people as possible, especially the younger people. Some of the college-age students would have received free scholarships to study in Russia had I continued on in my work here."

"But it looked as if you ran into a lot of opposition the last couple of weeks," spoke up Ken.

"That was my fault. I got a bit greedy and injected my own program to make some money. By the way, I will return it all. I have the names of the donors on my books. Because of the recent opposition, I was about ready to call on the Communist party in France to donate a couple of trucks for the area and even send in a shipment of used clothing. I know my people well enough to know that it would have quieted them down and given me time to withdraw my part of the program slowly. My Communist employers planned to give some items, but not nearly the amount that I promised the people. Somehow, Dr. Simms, I have to confess this whole thing to my fellow tribesmen, and I don't know how to do it."

"You have a lot of help, Martin," said Ken, smiling. "Chief Paul is well-known among the tribe, and I know that he will be a spokesman for you. You don't have to worry about the Christians; they will understand you. If the people get their money back, that will go a long way toward making them happy."

"I know that, Dr. Simms, but I feel so bad inside because of what I have done against them."

"The Lord knows all about it, Martin," said Marge. "He'll help you. No doubt you'll always have the scars of this on your mind."

"What about your membership in the Party?" asked Ken.

"I want to get back to France before I inform the Party of my break with them. You see, my wife is a member of the Party too."

Martin's answer shocked the missionaries. They now realized how deep Martin's problems were and how much they needed to pray for him.

"Regarding Bible school, I know what I have to do before I can think of that. Before I came this morning, it all seemed like an impossibility. Now, after talking with you folks, I can see that maybe, somewhere in the future, I might be able to get into the Lord's work. There is a lot to be done, though, before I can even apply, and the sooner I get at it, the better it will be. I want to leave immediately for the post. I will personally take back the money to each of my people, then I will go to the capital and take a plane back to France. You can give me the names and addresses of your missionaries, and I will make contact with them."

"If you don't mind, Martin," said Ken, "I will write to each of them as well and give them your name and address."

"Thank you, Dr. Simms. This talk has really helped me. I feel better already. I think I had better go see Chief Paul and then head back home."

"Oh, yes, it's time for me to go see Kondo," said Ken, walking with Martin to the door. "We surely appreciate your coming to see us and your sharing with us the things on your heart. We'll be praying for you, Martin."

The two men parted outside the door—Martin on his way to find Chief Paul and Ken to see his patient, Pastor Kondo.

"How is my best patient doing?" asked the doctor, looking down at the pastor.

"I'm feeling better all the time, Dr. Simms," responded Kondo, trying to smile. "Maybe I will not have to go to the capital hospital after all."

"I am afraid you will, Kondo," answered Ken. "You see, your legs are burned quite badly, and you will have to have some skin grafting done. That will eliminate most, if not all, of the scars you would normally have."

"You're the doctor," said Kondo. "I'm willing to do whatever you recommend for me."

"We should be able to leave tomorrow, Kondo. You are responding much faster than I thought you would. We'll travel slowly and stay the first night at the Bible school station. By doing that, we can take Tene back to school."

The few days spent at Yanga One had been very busy ones for the missionary couple. Ken had seen a number of sick people while Marge took advantage of their time there to teach many new songs to the villagers.

Wednesday morning found Kondo still improving and ready for the first part of the trip to the capital. Since they had to pass the mission station, Ken thought it best to unload some things and pick up other things for the trip. It was decided that Tessi would go along to the capital to care for Kondo while he was in the hospital.

With the supplies in the truck and the gas tank refilled, the pickup moved slowly down the long driveway to the main road. Even though he couldn't see them from where he lay in a suspended hammock, Pastor Kondo could hear the comments from the Christians lined up on both sides of the road. His heart was filled with praise to the Lord for being part of such a wonderful family—His family.

"There's Martin," said Marge, pointing to their friend standing in front of one of the small stores at the post. "He wants us to stop."

Ken pulled up alongside the smiling French-African.

"Hello, Martin. Did you have any problem getting back?"

"None at all, Dr. Simms. I just wanted you to know that the two women have returned to their villages. I am starting out today to take the money back to the villagers. The administrator wants to have a look at his region's garden situation, and I will be traveling

108

with him. I should be back in two days. In fact, he told me that he will be going to the capital on Friday of this week and will take me with him."

Tears came to Martin's eyes as he began his next words. "Dr. Simms, God has arranged all of this for me. There is a plane scheduled to leave Sunday afternoon, and I am planning to take it."

"Lord willing, Martin, Marge and I will be there to see you off. We have some shopping to do, so we will take advantage of this trip to get some of our supplies."

"I know you are in a hurry, my friends," said Martin, "but can we have prayer before you leave the post?"

"We surely can," Ken answered, stepping out of the truck.

A large number of people gathered about the truck and respectfully bowed their heads as Ken led in prayer. A chorus of amens echoed throughout the crowd as he finished. Martin climbed up on the side rack of the pickup and lightly patted Pastor Kondo on the shoulder.

"Good-bye, my brother. I'll come and see you at the hospital when I get to the capital. I'm praying for you."

"The Lord bless you, Martin," responded Kondo. "I thank the Lord for you."

As Ken closed the door, Martin moved closer to whisper something to him. "You will be happy to hear this, Dr. Simms. I gathered with several Christians last night at my house for Bible reading and prayer. What a wonderful change Jesus has made in my life. I truly am a new man."

23

Permission Granted

The trip to the Bible school station seemed to be the fastest and smoothest one yet for the Simmses. Of course, Tene had a big part in keeping everyone busy as he led singing nearly all the way.

"If that trip didn't do anything else," said Marge, laughing, "it took us through the songbook, and Tene got a lot of practice in song leading."

"That is one subject he should not fail," said Kondo, lying in the bedroom in his hammock. "I wondered when he was going to tire out, but he kept going from page to page."

Everyone laughed to hear Pastor Kondo join in the conversation, even though he still was a very sick man.

The Dykes had just finished their evening meal, but it was no problem for Bill and Kathy to get something ready for the five travelers. After the delicious meal, Tene bid farewell to Pastor Kondo and Tessi, assuring them of his prayers.

"Thank you, Dr. and Mrs. Simms, for providing the transportation for me to go to my grandmother's funeral. That was very kind of you." The young man shook hands and headed off down the path toward the students' dormitory. Ken stood shaking his head as he watched Tene go.

"And to think," he whispered to himself, "that that young man threw the spear that could have killed a co-worker."

The two couples started off early the next morning. Since the road seemed to get better as they neared the capital, Ken decided that he would ride with Kondo in the back while Marge did some of the driving. Tessi moved up into the cab with Marge. The heavy inner tube straps holding the hammock to its frame took all of the roughness out of the ride for the pastor. In fact, he mentioned a number of times how he was enjoying the trip.

Toward late afternoon, the pickup reached the smooth, black-top road of the city limits. Ken had changed with Marge several miles back in order to drive the truck through the capital city's traffic.

"I think I'll stop off at the mission station to let them know we're in town. We probably got here faster than any telegram could have possibly come."

Three miles inside the city limits, the pickup turned off the main road into the mission station driveway. Dale Banks was working under his car as the truck stopped in front of the house.

"Hi, Ken," Dale called, coming up out of the car pit. "Anything wrong?"

"Hello, Dale. I have Pastor Kondo in the back of the truck in a hammock. He got caught in a burning building last Sunday night and will need some grafting done. Right now, I want to get him to the hospital. I understand there are several new French doctors on the staff. This will give me a good opportunity to meet them."

Dorothy Banks came out while Ken and Dale were talking and began talking with Marge. The two couples walked over to the pickup so Kondo and Tessi could join in the conversation. It was decided that Ken and Dale would take Kondo to the hospital and Marge and Tessi would remain with Dorothy. This would give Tessi the opportunity to eat and get some rest. She would join Kondo later at the hospital.

The doctors at the hospital found the hammock to be such a good idea that they decided to carry the pastor to his room in it. Ken noted that the doctors were most cooperative and very understanding of the needs of his African brother.

"Those are bad burns, Dr. Simms," said one of the doctors, "but I've seen worse and they have healed well. I think we'll begin grafting tomorrow. Right now, there are some tests which we want to run."

Satisfied that Kondo was in the best hands possible, Ken said good-bye to his friend and left to return to the mission station. As the men arrived, they found a delicious meal ready for them. Tessi had eaten earlier and was fast asleep in a nearby room.

"She's gone through a lot lately," said Marge. "She's so quiet about everything, you would never know anything was wrong."

Later that evening, Ken and Marge took the pastor's wife to the hospital. Ken had arranged for an extra bed to be placed in the room beside Kondo. Tessi was delighted to see how their missionary friend had handled the details for their stay at the hospital.

"Thank you, Dr. Simms," she said in a whisper. "Thank you for all that you people have done for us. I am sure my husband would have died if you had not been there."

Back up-country, Martin had been busy caring for his matters. He made the trip with the region's administrator and found the people very happy to have their money returned to them. Nowhere did he find resentment against him for the false promises he had made. Deep within his heart Martin felt that someone had reached the people before him and prepared them for his visit. As he thought about this, a smile crossed his face. That someone could be none other than the village leader of Yanga One, Chief Paul. Again he saw the hand of God at work in his behalf.

When Friday morning's sun arose, there was a runner on his way to the region's administrator. He carried a message from Chief Paul, requesting transportation with the administrator to the capital city. What a pleasant surprise it was for Martin when the truck headed east toward Yanga One instead of south to the capital.

Back in the capital city, Ken was looking out the mission station window.

"It looks like rain out there," he commented.

"Don't you know by now, Ken, that it always rains on Saturday here in the capital?" kidded Dale Banks.

"I'm glad we were able to get most of our shopping done. I do have to check with the Minister of Health on Monday before we leave for home. I've requested permission to set up a small dispensary at Yanga One, and the official said that he would probably have the authorization letter for me by Monday morning. I haven't told Chief Paul about it yet, because I want to have the authorization for it first."

"That'll be a big surpise for him," said Dale. "How will you operate it and the one at Yanga Two at the same time?"

"I can't right now, but I can make periodic trips to Yanga One. I'm hoping I can train African Christians to help me operate the dispensary at Yanga One as well as the one at the station. Then, too, that would give the Yanga church a dispensary run by their own people."

Ken stopped for a moment, then continued. "I spoke with the chief surgeon at the hospital. He told me he could fit my medical personnel into their program very easily."

"That's wonderful, Ken," Dorothy exclaimed. "This would be a great help to you in your work."

"Exactly," said the doctor. "I get more excited every time I think about it."

"Oh, oh. Visitors," said Dale, getting up to look out the front door as a green military truck pulled up outside. Two men stepped from the cab.

"It's Chief Paul and that must be Martin Blanc," Dale said.

The two couples went outside quickly to greet their friends.

"What a surprise this is," said Ken, gripping the chief's hand.

"I had the opportunity to come, so I took advantage of it," responded the happy chief. "If you have room, perhaps I can return with you and Mrs. Simms."

"That sounds good to me, Chief," said Ken, turning to Martin Blanc. "And, Martin, how are you? It's good to see you again."

"Thank the Lord for the way things turned out. Everyone was happy to get their money back, and no one said anything about my promises to them. Of course, I had to tell each one what had happened to me. What great opportunities I had to tell them about Jesus and how He changed my life!"

"Come on in," called Dale. "We don't have to stand and talk in the driveway." The two men thanked the administrator's chauffeur, releasing him to return to the city. No sooner were they inside than it began to rain.

"If I remember correctly, Chief," said Ken, "it rained the last time we were here together."

"You're right, Dr. Simms. Kondo was with me too."

Kondo's name brought a serious tone to the conversation.

"How is Kondo?" Chief Paul asked. "I would like to go see him sometime this morning."

"He's doing fine, Chief Paul," answered Ken. "The French doctors working with him are some of the finest doctors I've seen anywhere. They have already done one skin graft. Kondo doesn't know much French, but he is sure getting the gospel message across to his doctors."

"I have to go to the airlines office," said Martin, "but maybe we can work something out for me to go to the hospital with you, Chief Paul. I would like to see Kondo this morning and, if at all possible, this afternoon too. Who knows? I might even have an opportunity to witness to his doctors."

Ken raised his finger to catch the chief's attention. "I'll take you and Martin in with me this morning, and then, if Martin needs transportation around to the various offices, I'll take him."

"Thank you, Dr. Simms," said Martin. "With your help, I think I can get everything done before noon."

As they were talking, Dorothy kept the coffee and cookies before them. The scene reminded the chief of his last visit when he and Pastor Kondo had asked Dr. and Mrs. Simms to come and be their missionaries in the Yanga area. The veteran leader thought of the big part his mother had played in asking Dr. and Mrs. Simms to come. A sadness swept over him as he thought of her.

"Let's be going," said Ken, standing up. "We've got a lot to do, and some of the offices will be closed this afternoon."

The morning went well. Pastor Kondo and Tessi were thrilled to see their visitors, and Martin was able to purchase space on the plane leaving the next day.

While Ken, Chief Paul and Martin were walking down a street, they met the Minister of Health. The government official informed Ken that he could pick up the authorization letter for the dispensary at Yanga One on Monday morning at nine o'clock.

"In fact," said the official, "if you are really pressed to return up-country, let me know and I will have one of my aides pick up the letter and bring it out to the mission station."

"Thank you, sir," said Ken. "I really appreciate your willingness to do that for me, but it won't be necessary. You see, I have a pastor friend in the hospital and I want to see him Monday morning before I start back up-country."

The official shook hands with the three men, expressing his pleasure in meeting Chief Paul and Martin. No sooner had he gone than Chief Paul turned to the missionary.

"Did my ears hear his words correctly, Dr. Simms?"

"What do you mean, Chief?"

"I thought I heard him say that he has given you permission to start a dispensary at Yanga One. Is that what he said?"

"You heard him right, Chief Paul," responded Ken. "I was going to surprise you on Monday by taking you to his office with me."

"I am glad it happened this way, Dr. Simms," said Martin, smiling. "I would not have heard about it for weeks."

"I never thought of that, Martin. I guess I was thinking only of surprising Chief Paul."

"Well, I know this may not mean anything, but my wife is a registered nurse. She works in a Paris hospital."

Chief Paul and Ken looked at each other. Somehow they felt that the preannounced surprise by the Minister of Health was scheduled by the Lord.

24

Good
News
from the
Mailbag

"Flight 128 is now ready for boarding. Please have your tickets ready for the attendant at the door."

Martin Blanc looked handsome in his navy blue suit. He reached out to begin the round of handshakes with his friends who had come to see him off. Standing between the two missionary couples was Chief Paul. Even Tessi was able to come and bid farewell to the man who had become a very dear friend to her and Kondo.

"Good-bye, Martin," she said, wiping the tears from her eyes with one hand while shaking his hand with the other. "Kondo and I will pray faithfully for you and Marie. We are asking God to save your dear wife."

"Thank you, Tessi. I have a deep love in my heart for you and Pastor Kondo. I hope the Lord will give us opportunity someday to fellowship together as Christian couples."

As Martin made his way to the plane, the group of believers was heavyhearted to see him leave. At the same time, they sensed the burden he was carrying, knowing he was returning home to a wife who did not share his love for Christ, a wife who could easily be the key to any future ministry for the Lord.

The huge plane lifted rapidly from the runway and climbed into the blue sky. The words and prayers of the Christians he left behind represented an indescribable joy and encouragement to the new Christian in the navy blue suit.

Monday morning, Ken, Marge and Chief Paul visited with

Kondo and Tessi. Kondo informed them that another skin graft surgery was scheduled for Friday. His spirits were high as he told of leading a man in the next room to Christ.

The missionaries picked up the authorization paper for the dispensary at Yanga One, stopped off at the mission station to say good-bye to Dale and Dorothy and then headed the pickup north. Conversation filled the cab as the three friends talked about the past as well as plans for the future.

"I can't get over the fact that Martin's wife is a nurse," said Marge.

"I could almost read Martin's thoughts when he told us about her there on the street," added Ken.

"Well, we are sure of one thing," chimed in Chief Paul. "We know that there are no surprises with the Lord. He knows the end from the beginning."

"I'll say amen to that, Chief," said Ken, staring ahead at the road.

The trip back to Yanga One was made without any trouble. The missionaries visited for about fifteen minutes and then headed back to Yanga Two. They were anxious to get back home. Even though the hour was late, a number of Christians from the workmen's village showed up to welcome them. When they finally got to bed, it was past midnight. But before dozing off, they prayed again for Kondo and the salvation of Marie Blanc. In a short time, both were sound asleep.

Two weeks later they received their first letter from Martin. Ken read it aloud to Marge as they sat in the front room of their home.

I called Marie from the airport and told her I was taking a taxi home. She was surprised to hear I was back in France. When I arrived at the apartment, I had a terrible feeling, knowing we were so very far apart in our beliefs, thinking, plans and goals. Everything was completely changed for me, and I knew I would have to pray for love and patience. As soon as I could, I sat down with Marie and explained to her what had happened to me. Naturally, she could not understand what I was telling her and thought I was either crazy or playing a joke on her.

During the next few days, Marie saw I was a changed man. I contacted Rev. and Mrs. Fine and they came over to visit us.

He and his wife made a tremendous impression on Marie. She is showing some interest as she is beginning to think that, perhaps, communism is not the answer. Please continue to pray for her as well as for me. I will keep in touch with you.

Your brother in the Lord, Martin.

P.S. I resigned from the Party the day after I arrived home. I am now working as a salesman in a large clothing store.

Ken made several trips to Yanga One the next couple of weeks, hauling building supplies. The Christians decided they would take up a collection and purchase aluminum to use as roofing for the chapel. There was no lack of workers as the people swarmed like bees over the structure. In two days' time the men had the new roof on their chapel.

"That looks great, Chief Paul," Ken said as he stood beside his African friend. The shining aluminum reflected the bright sunlight, causing the men to shade their eyes.

"Yes, and it is one more step in making the Lord's work even stronger here at Yanga One. When people work and pray together, they become closer to each other. We need to band together as believers and learn as much about God's Word as we can. Martin's short stay among us taught us all a good lesson."

"I hope there's a letter from Martin when I get home," said Ken. "I'm anxious to hear if our missionaries in France were able to talk with Marie."

"We're all praying, Dr. Simms," replied Chief Paul.

That evening as Ken parked the truck in front of the garage, he saw Marge come running out the back door of the house with something in her hand. He knew she had good news by the look on her face.

"What a mail day this has been," she called, running up to the truck.

"Who'd we hear from, Honey?" Ken asked, putting his arm around his wife and giving her a big hug.

"Well, let's see," she said teasingly. "We got a letter from Kondo and Tessi. Here's one from Dale and Dorothy, and here's one from Mr. and Mrs. Martin Blanc."

"How's Kondo? And what's the news on Marie?"

"You're going to have to read them yourself," said Marge, laughing. "But you can read them to me. I promise I'll be a good listener!"

The couple walked quickly into the house and sat down in the living room. Ken took the letters, opened the one from Martin and Marie, and began to read:

Dear Friends in Christ,

I have good news for you. Marie is now a Christian. This past week, Dan and Alice Fine came over for a meal. Alice and Marie spent a long time together talking about the Lord. The Fines then invited us to church on Sunday morning and asked us to have the noon meal with them. Marie listened to every word Dan said in his message. Later on, around the table, we talked some more about God and His love for us. After we arrived back in our apartment, Marie asked me if I would pray with her.

Thank the Lord, I had the joy of seeing my wife come to accept Jesus as her Savior. We called Dan and Alice and they came right over.

Dr. and Mrs. Simms, life is worth living for us as a couple! It is wonderful to know that we trust in the same Savior. Thank you for praying. God has answered.

Ken stopped to clear his throat. Tears swelled up in his eyes. "It's unbelievable, Marge. It's just unbelievable."

"It's true, Honey. Martin and Marie Blanc, former Communists, are now Christians."

Ken opened the letter from Pastor Kondo and began to read:

I cannot write very well yet, but I think you will be able to read this. I have had my third operation and the doctor tells me I can leave here in one more week.

Ken looked up at the wall calendar. "That means he's leaving the hospital about now. He wrote the letter a week ago."

Ken continued reading:

Mr. Banks said he would also write to you. I think he may come up to visit you in two weeks. If he does, he said he will bring Tessi and me with him in order to save you a trip. It will be good to see you all again. Thank you for your prayers."

Excitedly, Ken opened the letter from his co-workers.

We will probably be up to visit you in about two weeks. I talked with the doctor today, and he is very pleased with Kondo's recovery. He is healing beautifully. He should be leaving the hospital in about a week. We will care for him here at the mission station. I'll send you a telegram telling you when I plan to arrive. I hope you receive it.

"Wow!" exclaimed Ken through a wide grin. "Praise the Lord. Marie's saved and Kondo's coming home. That's almost too much to take in one day."

"The Lord has a lot more blessings for us, Honey," called Marge as she made her way into the kitchen. "It hardly seems possible that the same Martin Blanc who lived over there in the apartment is the one who wrote us from France telling us that he and his wife are now both saved."

"I know what you mean, Marge," replied Ken, following her into the kitchen. "But it's real, every bit of it, including the sad parts, such as Becky's illness and death, Kota's accident and Bio's heart attack. Then, too, Kondo's accident."

"It's amazing how God has brought glory to Himself through all of these things," added Marge.

That night before he went to bed, Ken wrote a long letter to Martin and Marie. He told them how happy he and Marge were to learn of Marie's salvation.

"We are praying that God will give you direction for your lives," he concluded. "Please write soon. We are anxious to hear from you and the Lord's blessings upon you."

Later, as he drifted off to sleep, little did Ken realize that at that very hour Paul Davis was sitting in the mission's headquarters in Cleveland, Ohio, talking about his return to Africa.

"I know it will be difficult, Dr. Linsay, but I believe God wants me to return to Africa."

"When do you want to return, Paul?" the mission's president asked.

"I'd like to return in about six months, sir. That would give me time to raise my passage and purchase some necessary items."

"We'll be praying with you, Paul, concerning this. It will be a lonely life for you, but I'm convinced you know what God's will is for you."

Meanwhile, in France, Dan and Alice Fine had just left the Blanc apartment. In the course of the conversation, both Martin and Marie asked if they could be baptized and join the church. The thing that stuck in the missionaries' minds more than anything else was something that Marie had asked them as they were leaving. As she shook Dan's hand, she asked, "Since I'm a nurse, Dan, is there any possibility of using my nursing skill for God's work—for example, in Africa?"

A week later, along with the arrival of Kondo, Tessi and Dale and Dorothy Banks at Yanga Two, would come the mail sack. Inside would be a letter from Paul Davis and one from Martin and Marie—both letters involving Africa.

25

A
God-given
Privilege

The sound of the horn brought Marge Simms running from the house. "Dorothy! Dale! It's so good to see you. Where are Kondo and Tessi?"

"We dropped them off in the workmen's village. Kondo was weary from the trip, and we saw no reason to bring him here when he was so tired," answered Dale.

"Is he all right?" asked Marge.

"Oh, yes, he's just fine," responded Dale. "I knew he was tired, and asked him if he would like to get out over there. He said he would, so I stopped near his house."

"Ken's up at Yanga One. He should be back any minute," Marge told her co-workers. "Chief Paul wanted to be here when Kondo arrived. I think the village of Yanga One is going to do something special for Pastor Kondo and Tessi. They won't even tell Ken and me as they want it to be a surprise for us too."

The missionaries went into the house to get out of the hot, afternoon sun. Marge poured them each a glass of fresh grapefruit juice.

"I really appreciate these fruit trees the earlier missionaries planted around the station. This fruit is worth its weight in gold," she commented.

About an hour later, the Simms's blue pickup turned down the driveway from the main road. Chief Paul sat beside Ken on the front seat. Marge, Dorothy and Dale went out to greet the arrivals from Yanga One.

"It is wonderful to see you again," said Chief Paul, shaking Dale's and Dorothy's hands. "Tomorrow the people from Yanga

One are coming to pay a special tribute to Pastor Kondo. Some of them are walking on the road this very moment."

That evening the people began to arrive. Chief Paul, along with several others, occupied the apartment. Many of the people were taken in by families in the workmen's village. Others stretched out on the brick benches in the church building. There seemed to be people everywhere, and by the time morning came Yanga Two took on the appearance of a holiday festival. Since the church could not begin to hold the people, it was decided that they would meet in the large front yard of the mission station. Pastor Kondo walked slowly to a special cushioned chair reserved for him. Chief Paul took charge of the meeting. Chairs were lined up alongside Kondo's chair for the missionaries.

"First of all, we are going to sing some hymns," Chief Paul announced. "Then the Word of God will be read by our missionary, Dr. Simms."

The blend of voices made tears come to Marge's eyes. It was difficult for her to sing because of the lump that formed in her throat.

After several hymns, Chief Paul asked Ken to read. The doctor read 2 Corinthians 5:19-21 and 1 Thessalonians 4:13-18. The chief then turned to Dale Banks and asked him to pray. A series of amens could be heard from the crowd as Dale finished praying. Chief Paul then stood up to speak.

"My friends, this is a special day for us from Yanga One. To go back and try to tell all that has happened both at Yanga One and here at Yanga Two this past year would take many, many hours. We are convinced that God has dealt with us in ways we will never forget. There have been some very wonderful and blessed events as well as some difficult times. I personally believe that God has given us a great victory, and there are tremendous days of blessing ahead for us as we walk with the Lord."

A clicking of tongues indicated that the people were in agreement with what their chief was saying.

"After my mother, Bio, accepted Jesus as her Savior, she became the spiritual mother of Yanga One. Our hearts were mixed with both sadness and gladness when God called her Home. When our chapel building caught fire, your pastor did something that we will never forget. He risked his life to save the casket and body of my mother. The doctors did a good job on him, but he still bears the scars from that night."

The chief looked down at the pastor. It was difficult for him to speak as the emotion of the hour overwhelmed him.

"Pastor Kondo, my people want to do something special for you and Tessi. So you will never have to fear fire in your house, we are going to build you a new house with an aluminum roof. It will be divided into rooms just like Dr. Simms's house."

Tears flowed down Kondo's face as the chief spoke.

"We are going to furnish your house for you, too, Pastor Kondo. One of the rooms will be a spare bedroom so I will be able to stay with you when I visit this village."

The chief's remark brought laughter from the crowd.

"My men want to begin construction immediately. There is a shipment of aluminum and lumber at the post, and we have already put a hold on it for your house."

Chief Paul stopped to give Pastor Kondo the opportunity to respond. The pastor slowly rose to his feet. He stood in silence for some time before he began to speak.

"My dear people," he said in a broken voice, "I cannot find the words to say to you that would express the thanks that Tessi and I have in our hearts. You are all so good to us, but I want to give the credit for it all to the One Who deserves it. It is only because of Jesus that we meet like this today. There was a time when we hated and fought each other. Yes, some even ate their enemies. Thanks be to God Who brought His precious Word to us by the hands of our missionaries. I give Him the praise today for all that He has done for us. Thank you, dear friends, for your gift to us. We will always appreciate your kindness and thoughtfulness."

The pastor stood for a moment after he had finished speaking and then sat down. Chief Paul rose once again to speak to the people.

"Thank you, Pastor Kondo. We thank the Lord for your leadership among us, and for the love and patience you have shown to us in many ways. It is a privilege for us to do this for you and your wife."

Chief Paul then closed the meeting in prayer. As Ken listened to him pray, his thoughts went back to the night he stayed with the chief in the apartment. Again 2 Corinthians 5:17 came to mind as he thought of the changed life of his African friend.

When the chief finished praying, he announced there would be refreshments. Unknown to the villagers and missionaries of Yanga Two, the chief had purchased coffee, tea and boxes of cookies from one of the small stores at the post. For the greater part of the crowd, there were roasted manioc roots, peanut butter rolls and roasted peanuts. The food had been prepared in secret in a nearby village.

"He's something else," said Dale, helping himself to a peanut butter roll. "God has really used that man here in the Yanga area."

"Yes, He has," replied Ken. "Chief Paul is one of the dearest friends I have."

Toward evening, the crowd began to disappear, making its way slowly back to Yanga One. As Ken and Dale stood on the front porch talking over the day's happenings, a soldier on a bicycle entered the driveway from the main road.

"He's carrying a sack on the back. It must be the mail," spoke Ken, going out to the driveway to meet the approaching bicyclist.

"Hello, there, what do you have?" Ken called.

"It's your mail, Dr. Simms. Mr. Banks dropped the bag off yesterday at the administrator's office, but we were not able to sort it right away. We found out that Chief Paul was having something special for you today, so the administrator decided to hold your mail until your meeting was over."

"Thank you," Ken said to the soldier. "I'll empty the sack right away so you can take it back with you."

As Ken dumped the contents of the bag on a table on the front porch, his eyes immediately saw the name Davis on one of the letters. He had a good idea what the letter said. The soldier neatly folded the bag, placed it on the back of his bicycle, and started back to the post. Dale told Ken and Marge to go ahead and read their mail. He and Dorothy would take a walk around the mission station.

"Listen to this, Honey," said Ken, holding Paul's letter before him.

> I know it may seem strange for me to want to return to Africa alone and so soon after Becky's Home-going. My heart is there in Africa, and I believe that God wants me to come back. Lord willing, I plan to return in about six months. Please continue to pray for me as I do for you. My love to you all. Please greet Kondo and Chief Paul for me.

"It'll be good to have Paul back with us again," said Ken. "He's such a good missionary and has a heart of love for the Africans."

"I'm glad he's coming back," added Marge. "Maybe we'll be able to establish another work up north after he gets here."

Ken opened the next letter which was from Martin and Marie. The more he read, the more excited he became.

> We had a long talk with Dan and Alice yesterday. I know this will be a surprise to you, but we talked about Bible school. Marie and I have joined the church that Dan pastors and we love the people. Marie was the first to say something when she asked Dan if God could use her nurses' training. She mentioned Africa when she spoke to him. This was all new to me, but I can assure you, it was good news. Dan and Alice are very helpful to us. They told of a Bible institute which your mission operates in northeast France. We are taking a ride over next week to visit it. I can hardly believe that this has all happened to us. All I can say is, "Thank the Lord!" He did it all. By the way, I want to ask this before I close. I know we are probably four or five years away from working as missionaries there in Africa, but do you think there is a place for us? The thoughts of being missionaries among my own people keep increasing every day. Please tell me what you think of our coming down to work with you. We send our love in the Lord.
>
> Your Brother and Sister in Christ,
> Martin and Marie

"Oh, Ken, that's wonderful," said Marge, wiping her eyes. "Wouldn't it be great having Martin and Marie as co-workers? And to think, she's a nurse too."

Ken took Marge by the hand and started out the door. "Let's share this with Dale and Dorothy, and then we can walk over to the workmen's village and tell Kondo and Chief Paul the good news."

"Would you please read that about Mr. Davis over again, Dr. Simms?" asked Pastor Kondo. "I want my ears to hear it once more."

Ken reread Paul's letter for the third time. No sooner had he finished than Chief Paul spoke up.

"And would you read the one from Martin for me again? That news is so good, I do not know if there is room for all of it to fit inside my heart at one time. Dr. Simms, this is another great day for the Banda people."

Ken read the letter from Martin and Marie. Chief Paul just sat, slowly shaking his head from side to side.

"I can hardly wait to see them all. Just think, to have Mr. Davis, Martin and Marie, and you dear friends here living among us."

The village leader hesitated a moment and then continued. "But we cannot forget the responsibilities that we have for today and tomorrow and the days and weeks to come. There is still much to be done, and God has privileged us to have a part in doing it."

"You're so right, Chief Paul," said Ken, reaching out to shake his friend's hand. "God has privileged us to have a part in doing it."